A Dictionary of Reptiles and Amphibians

by *Rube Allyn*

GREAT OUTDOORS PUBLISHING CO. Not Inc.

4747 28th Street No.

St. Petersburg, Florida 33714

Foreword

Back in 1952 the first edition of the Dictionary of Reptiles was published as the second volume of the Red Cover series of nature books. Like its predecessor, the Dictionary of Fishes, the reptile edition was produced to serve as a layman's guide to identification of the creatures we see around us.

The publishers and the author look back with pride to know that in this time the Dictionary has traveled around the world to 50,000 homes to become an accepted standard for study. Since the first edition was printed, many new records have come to light—and much more information has been included.

This interest in nature and the quest for more knowledge has been exceedingly gratifying to the author. The helpful contributions from Herpetologists around the world has added much to the storehouse of information on this subject. For this assistance a heartfelt thanks.

In truth this book has been written by outdoorsmen themselves. It was those questions propounded to the author as outdoor editor of The St. Petersburg Times, which have made it possible to search out the answers and set them down on these pages. The very number of queries indicated how much demand there is for a book such as this.

Some 400 representative members of the reptile clan are presented for observation. The average size and extreme size is furnished, as well as identifying colors and poisonous characteristics. Facts of their lives, such at reproduction—and details of close identification, desired by a person involved in serious study, must be obtained from the excellent scientific books on this subject.

Information on points of size, color and habitat of reptiles published in this book is largely obtained from the findings of America's foremost Herpetologists. For their intensive study and devotion to the seeking of knowledge for the good of mankind we humbly pay reverence.

Our information gained from study of reptiles since 1932, while on duty with the St. Petersburg Times, we glady contribute to the store of world knowledge. To all who study the lives of reptiles, we offer this new information, added to a summary of the old. Take what you wish, use it for advantage to mankind.

Especial gratitude for information is extended to R. L. Ditmars, Litt. D., who before passing to his reward reached a height of fame seldom equalled in the scientific world; Karl P. Schmidt, D. Dwight Davis, Albert A. Enzenbacher, Roger Conant, E. G. Boulenger and Percy A. Morris, all scientists of world-wide fame.

The 29 Kinds of Living Crocodilians

Species		Found	Adult Length
American Alligator	*Alligator mississipiensis*	S. E. U.S.A.	16 ft. 2 in.
Chinese Alligator	*Alligator sinensis*	East China	6½ ft.
Spectacled Caiman	*Caiman crocodilus crocodilus*	South America	7 ft.
Rio Apaporis Caiman	*Caiman crocodilus apaporiensis*	Colombia, S.A.	6 ft.
Brown Caiman	*Caiman crocodilus fuscus*	Colombia to Mexico	6 ft.
Jacare	*Caiman crocodilus yacare*	Paraguay, South America	7 ft.
Broad-nosed Caiman	*Caiman latirostris*	Brazil and Paraguay	7 ft.
Black Caiman	*Melanosuchus niger*	Amazon drainage, South America	12 ft.
Dwarf Caiman	*Paleosuchus palpebrosus*	Amazon and the Guianas	4 ft.
Smooth-fronted Caiman	*Paleosuchus trigonatus*	Amazon Drainage	5 ft.
American Crocodile	*Crocodylus acutus*	Florida, Central America, Mexico, West Indies	15 ft.
Orinoco Crocodile	*Crocodylus intermedius*	Orinoco River, S.A.	19 ft.
River Crocodile	*Crocodylus acutus lewyanus*	Colombia, S.A.	10 ft.
Sharp-nosed Crocodile	*Crocodylus cataphractus*	W. & Central Africa	8 ft.
Johnstone's Crocodile	*Crocodylus johnstonei*	North Australia	8 ft.
Morelet's Crocodile	*Crocodylus moreleti*	Yucatan to Guatemala	8 ft.
Nile Crocodile	*Crocodylus niloticus*	Africa and Israel	16 ft.
New Guinea Crocodile	*Crocodylus n. novae-guineae*	New Guinea	9 ft.
Mindoro Crocodile	*Crocodylus n. mindorensis*	Philippine Islands	8 ft.
Saltwater Crocodile	*Crocodylus porosus porosus*	Asia, Australia	25 ft.
Ceylonese Saltwater Crocodile	*Crocodylus porosus*	Minikana, Ceylon	12 ft.
Cuban Crocodile	*Crocodylus rhombifer*	Cuba and Isle Of Pines	10 ft.
Siamese Crocodile	*Crocodylus siamensis*	Borneo, Siam, Java	12 ft.
West African Dwarf	*Crocodile Osteolamus tetraspis tetraspis*	West Africa	6 ft.
Congo Dwarf Crocodile	*Osteolamus tetraspis osborni*	Africa	4 ft.
Mugger Crocodile	*Crocodylus palustris palustris*	India & Pakistan	13 ft.
Ceylonese Mugger	*Crocodylus palustris kimbula*	Ceylon	12 ft.
False Gavial	*Tomistoma schlegeli*	Malay Peninsula, Sumatra and Borneo	16 ft.
Gavial	*Gavialis gangeticus*	India	21 ft.

Alligators and Caiman

● CHINESE ALLIGATOR *Alligator sinensis*

Average size 4 feet; largest 6 feet.

Dull black with irregular dull yellow cross bands. No webs between toes distinguishes this species.

A night-roving and day-sleeping Oriental inhabitant of the Chinese rivers. A docile creature, not known to attack or even bite the natives. An unusual angle is the belief by Buddhist priests that the alligators are beneficial to man and consider it a virtuous act to befriend them when found in the hands of captors. In spite of this, they are an endangered species. Why? One report has it that "people are eating them up".

Range: Lower Yangtze Valley of China.

● BROAD-NOSED CAIMAN *Caimen latirostris*

Average size 4½ feet; largest 7 feet.

Hard to distinguish from alligator, except has eyelids, greatly enlarged, which look like horns. Short, broad nose. Alligator has a black body with yellow markings; caiman has a tan body with black markings.

A mean-tempered and vicious creature of the crocodile family. Seldom giving up to docile captivity. Feeds on fish mostly.

Range: Brazil and Paraguay.

● SPECTACLED CAIMAN *Caiman c. crocodilus*

Also called BABILLA.

Average size 4 feet; largest 8 feet; dangerous to man.

Recognized by markings on the head resembling spectacles.

Smallest of the crocodiles, seen in Panama and throughout Central America. A good source of leather for native leather workers.

The native uses a unique method of capture. He lashes two pointed sticks crosswise, attaches a rope—tying the free end around his waist. Walking waist deep into the river, he gently slaps the water in imitation of an animal drinking. The croc rises and makes for the native's extended arm. The hunter jams the stick into the croc's mouth and makes for shore.

Although its broad snout looks like a 'gator, the caiman is an entirely different creature.

Range: Central and South America.

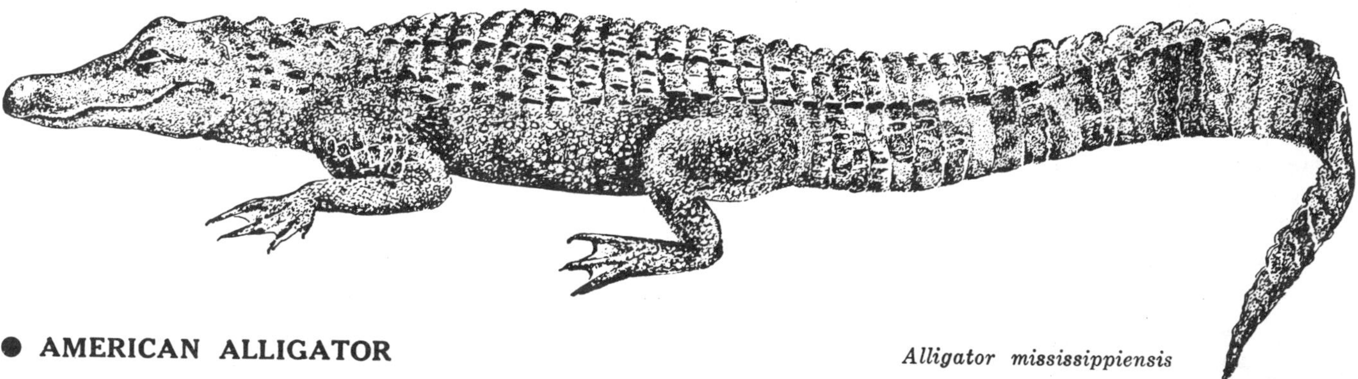

● AMERICAN ALLIGATOR *Alligator mississippiensis*

Largest in Florida, 14 feet, 7 inches at Ross Allen's Reptile Institute, Silver Springs, named "Big George". Largest known specimen 19 feet and 2 inches, killed by E. A. McIlhenny, Sr., Louisiana naturalist. Black body color, yellowish to white on belly.

There is much discussion of how large alligators grow, but for all practical purposes an 11-foot one is very big. They are not especially dangerous up to 8 feet, but beware of any 'gator on a nest. They are most active at the 8 to 10 foot stage and at this period can be considered dangerous. Beyond this, the larger they become, the more docile and less active. Only two places on earth have alligators, the Southern United States and China.

Crocodiles

● **AMERICAN CROCODILE** *Crocodylus acutus*

Largest known in Florida or America, 17 feet according to Ross Allen.

Black on top, yellowish on sides and white on belly. The crocodile is more slender and agile than the alligator. Its long, pointed head at once distinguishes it.

The crocodile is the world's largest reptile and probably the most vicious. The jaws, pointed with a slight hump on the nose are fitted with vicious teeth. A sure way to identify a crocodile is to look for two notches on either side of the upper jaw, permitting the lower canines to pierce the bony upper jaw and glisten in the sun above the dark skin of the snout. The canines may not protrude but the notches are always present. Not so with the alligator, he has no notches and only bares his canines when he opens his mouth.

Young crocodiles are distinctly greenish, with black markings. Young adults are olive, while the very old are dull gray. The olive and gray colors distinguish the crocodile from the black, blue-black of the alligator. Young alligators are distinctively black with yellow crossbands.

A savage beast, comparable to the Orinoco Crocodile of South America. They attack and devour most anything they can catch. Have a fast movement and particularly powerful tail, used to swing and knock a victim into position for the snapping jaws.

American Crocodiles are rare in Florida. They are found only between Cape Sable and Key Largo on the lower tip of Florida. The area around Lake Surprise being a classic location. Originally found as far north as Lake Worth, with many specimens living in Miami's Biscayne Bay in the 1800's. They now are found mostly in tropical America and the Greater Antilles. Both the Atlantic and Pacific tropical coasts are home to the American Crocodile.

Average size 12 feet; largest 25 feet; highly dangerous.

● **NILE CROCODILE** *Crocodylus niloticus*

Average length 14 feet; largest 18 feet, according to Ditmar. Very dangerous to man.

Dark olive-green, fierce jagged teeth.

The Nile Crocodile is one of the oldest recorded animals. Is referred to in the Bible as "Leviathan." A fierce and cruel animal, will attack anything on sight, often rushing from the water to attack a victim on the river bank.

Considerable mythology has been built around them and in many primitive countries they are worshipped as gods. The saying "he sheds crocodile tears" comes from the fact that they actually shed tears while eating a man. The pressure of jaws cause the lachrymal glands to compress and the tears flow.

Range: Through Palestine, Madagascar and all of Africa.

● **SALT WATER CROCODILE** *Crocodylus porosus*

Average size 12 feet; largest 20 feet; highly dangerous.

The most dangerous of all crocodiles, including the Nile species. Inhabits the rivers and bays of East Indian rivers. Has been seen swimming in the ocean more than 100 miles from shore.

Because of their size, are more than a match for any other creature. Will attack on sight any animal they can catch. Will pursue humans anywhere they are sighted.

Range: From Ceylon to the Philippines.

Crocodiles and Gavials

● WEST AFRICAN DWARF CROCODILE

Osteolaemus tetraspis tetraspis

Average size 4 feet; largest 6 feet; not dangerous.

Darker color than other crocodiles, has a thinner tail and a shorter, broader snout. Eyes larger and slightly more elevated.

A pigmy crocodile found in a limited area. Not vicious as others, but will show temper if annoyed. Natives value the hide for spear shields. In many ways, resembles an alligator. A close relative is the Congo Dwarf Crocodile.

Range: West Africa.

● SHARP-NOSED CROCODILE

Crocodylus cataphractus

Average size 6 feet; largest 8 feet; dangerous.

Distinguishing feature, very narrow snout, on the order of a gavial.

Although a vicious crocodile, as are all the African members of the family, this species does not grow to the enormous length of the Nile crocodiles. Its flattened snout is better equipped to catch fish than mammals. They prefer the ponds and the brackish pools of the forest, near a river.

Range: West and Central Africa.

● MALAYAN GAVIAL

Tomistoma schlegeli

Also called FALSE GAVIAL.

Average size 15 feet; largest 16 feet.

Greenish-brown. Recognized by long slender snout.

Somewhat shorter snout than the Indian Gavial and the closest link between the gavials and the crocodiles. Has a fairly docile disposition usually, however there have been many instances of attack on man.

Feed mostly on fish, which they catch by a quick snapping of jaws. Will not refuse birds and small mammals if they are handy.

Range: The rivers of India, also Sumatra and Borneo.

● INDIAN GAVIAL

Gavialis gangeticus

Also called GHARIAL.

Average size 15 feet; largest 30 feet.

Greenish-brown, distinguished by long snout.

Probably the largest of the crocodiles, yet entirely fish-eating. Is not known to attack larger mammals, although birds and small mammals may be eaten. Not known to attack man.

Feeds by lying motionless in the water for hours, then when fish swim past, swishes long, thin jaws sideways to trap them. Likes to lie on the bank and bask in the sun on Winter days.

Range: Inhabits India.

Monitors

● KOMODO DRAGON
Varanus komodoensis

Average size of full-grown lizard is 12 feet and weighs 300 pounds; dangerous.

Fairly smooth skin. A giant of the lizard family.

Found on the East Indian Island of Koodo, now made a game preserve by the Dutch government. Quite ferocious in wild state, but becomes docile in captivity.

When young they climb trees and when older they swim, catching turtles. They can kill a deer or pig. Have a heavy set of saw-tooth teeth, a long yellowish tongue which can dart out at great lengths. A formidable looking creature.

In captivity they are fed once every five days, mostly on fowl or eggs.

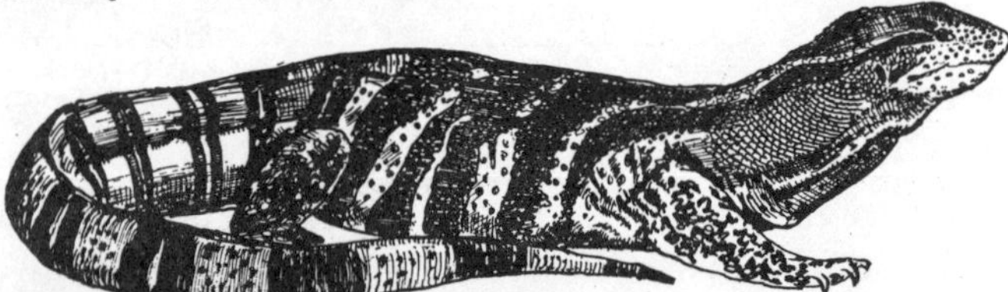

WHITE-THROATED MONITOR
Varanus albigularis

Average length 3½ feet; largest 5 feet; harmless.

Grayish-brown above with large, round spots in dark-edged yellow arranged in transverse series on the back. Rather large head and short neck.

Lives usually along the river bank and enjoys searching out the eggs of other reptiles. Takes to low trees whenever possible, but will be found in water or on land. Travels equally well on both.

Range: Southern Africa.

● NILE MONITOR
Varanus niloticus

Average size 5 feet; largest 8 feet.

Blackish, leathery skin, some yellowish blotches.

Second largest of the monitors. Is carnivorous —and in the wild state will rush a human if disturbed, or unable to escape. They have a very long forked tongue and sharp teeth which can inflict a bad wound. Their method of attack is to rush, turn sidewise and whip out with their tail.

Range: Northeast Africa.

● LACE MONITOR
Varanus varius

Average size 4½ feet; largest 6 feet; harmless.

Identified by unusually large head scales. Brownish with white stripes around forefeet. Hind feet have white dots. Tail exceptionally long.

A tree-dwelling monitor of unusually large size. In spite of exceptional size this creature can move about in the trees at a fast pace. There have been rumors of species up to 9 feet in length, never verified.   Range: Australia.

● BANDED MONITOR
Varanus salvator

Average size 6 feet; largest 9 feet; harmless.

Brown above with yellow spots and bands on the sides of the body.

Frequents marshy localities or climbs into the low branches of trees. Hunts and eats small mammals and birds. Has a habit of diving from the trees into water when disturbed. Burrows in the banks of rivers for nest building.

Range: Malay Peninsula, South China.

 # Giant Iguanas 

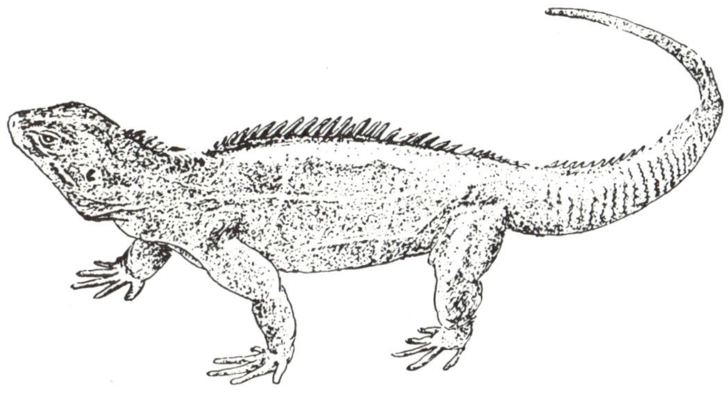

● ISLAND IGUANA
Cyclura carinata

Average length 24 inches; largest 3 feet; edible; harmless.

Pale pinkish-gray, marked with black bars on the sides. A row of soft, lance-like spines cover neck and back. They sometimes weigh up to 30 pounds.

This lizard is used extensively for food in South America and the West Indies. Although they spend a good deal of time in trees, they also swim. Their home is a burrow in a river bank. Eggs are sought and eaten by South Americans.

Range: South America and the West Indies.

● RHINOCEROS IGUANA
Metopcero cornutus

Average length 3 feet; largest 4½ feet; dangerous.

Dark brown in color with three horns on the snout about three-eighths of an inch in length.

This lizard looks a good deal like a pre-historic mammal. Often squats for hours on its hind quarters when not interested in fighting or eating. Greatest occupational enterprise is fighting. It can inflict as much damage as a wildcat if approached. However, when grabbed by the hind legs, it is powerless. In captivity it becomes tame.

Food most desired is chicken or small mammals and most any kind of vegetables.

Range: Porto Rico and Haiti.

● GALAPAGOS MARINE IGUANA
Amblyrhynchus cristatus

Average size 3½ feet; largest 5 feet; harmless.

Dull black and brown. No markings.

A sea-going lizard, living on land in the darkness and spending much time in the sea in daylight. Usually travel in groups of several hundred. They have no enemies on land and possibly only one—the shark—in the water. They are not afraid of man and can be approached and even tormented without a show of temper.

Range: Only on the Galapagos Islands.

● GALAPAGOS LAND IGUANA
Conolophus subcristatus

Average size 4 feet; largest 5 feet; harmless.

Grayish-brown with scales that appear speckled.

Somewhat like the Marine Iguanas in appearance, except the land cousin does not go near the water. Only moisture he sees is that taken from the cactus plant. Ordinarily gentle-mannered, yet will anger much quicker than the marine relative.

Feeds chiefly on berries and cactus leaves and the sprouts of acacia trees. It sometimes climbs trees to feed. Seldom fights, except in captivity.

Lives in burrows dug in eroded limestone, scratched out in a lazy manner.

Range: Only on the Galapagos Islands.

 # Iguanas and Others 

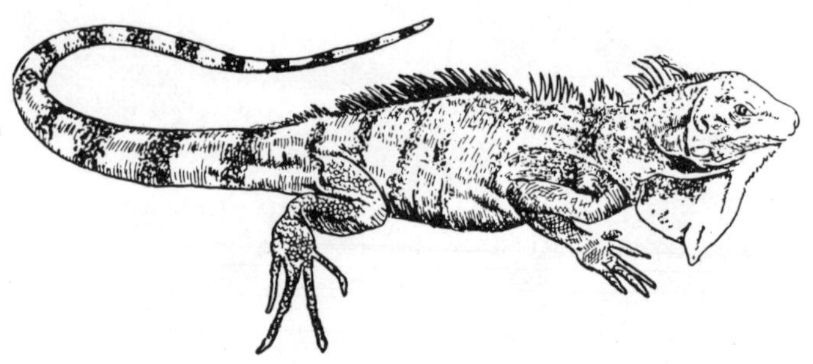

● **GREEN IGUANA** *Iguana iguana*

Average size 4 feet; largest 6 feet; harmless; edible.

Pale greenish-gray, marked on the sides with bold black bars. On the tail there are broad black rings.

A tree-dwelling creature, despite the large size. They may be seen lying on tree boughs with their legs hanging over, or on top of telegraph poles. Although mostly dining on vegetation, they will consume almost anything from small mammals to eggs. Are esteemed for food value and hunted continuously by natives.

Range: Mexico, Central America and the West Indies.

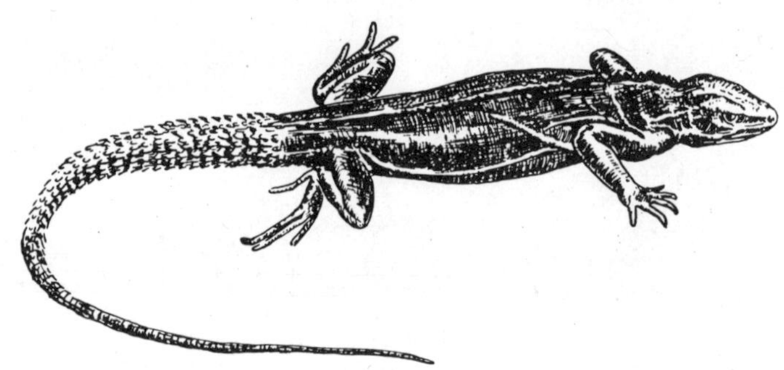

● **SPINY-TAILED IGUANA**

Ctenosaura s. simile

Average size 24 inches; largest 4 feet; harmless.

Identified by round tail, covered with spines. Used as a weapon.

This over-size lizard is a bad-looking fellow. Has a hide like leather, loosely fitted on the body. Is more of an aggressive type than some of his brothers. Likes to catch birds and small mammals, although will eat vegetables, too.

Range: Mexico and Central America.

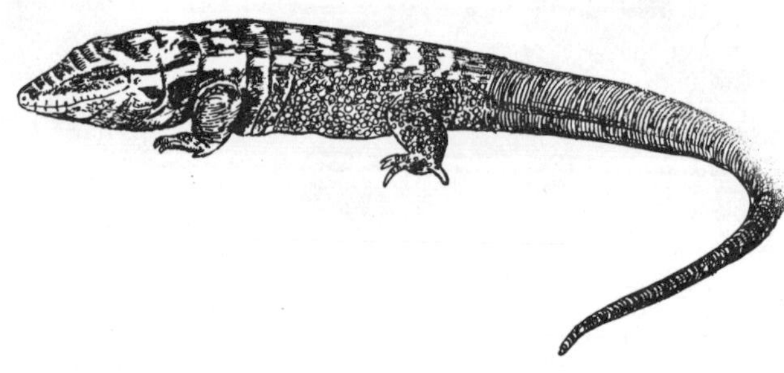

● **RED TEGU** *Tupinambis rufescens*

Average size 3 feet; largest 3 feet, 6 inches; harmless.

Reddish above with brown transverse bands. Lower parts more or less distinct irregular dark blotches.

One of the largest of the American lizards. They are quite docile and make good pets. Can be released in a room and caught at will. Quite similar to the Monitors in their behavior.

Like to eat eggs and will capture small mammals.

Range: Argentine, South America.

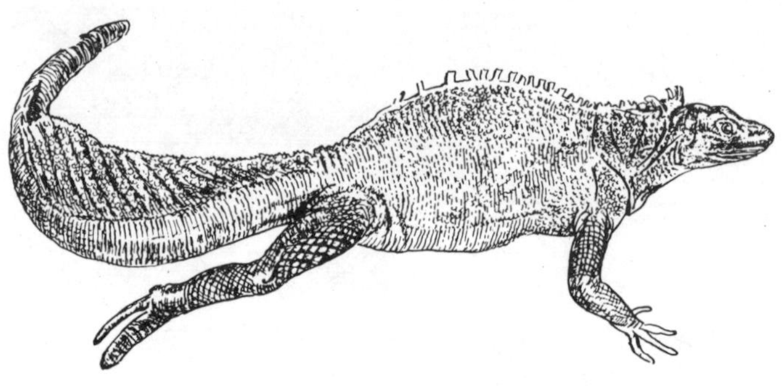

● **ARMED SAIL-TAILED LIZARD** *Acanthosuara armata*

Average size 2 feet; largest 3 feet; harmless.

Distinguished by large erectile tissue on tail in form of a sail.

A dry land and desert-loving lizard, capable of climbing trees as well as fast movement over arid ground. Will give the appearance of a fight when cornered but does not bite unless severely harmed.

Range: Southeastern Asia.

Tegus and Tuatara

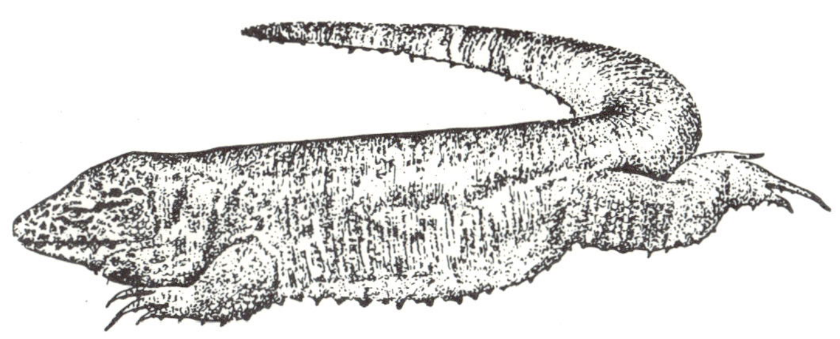

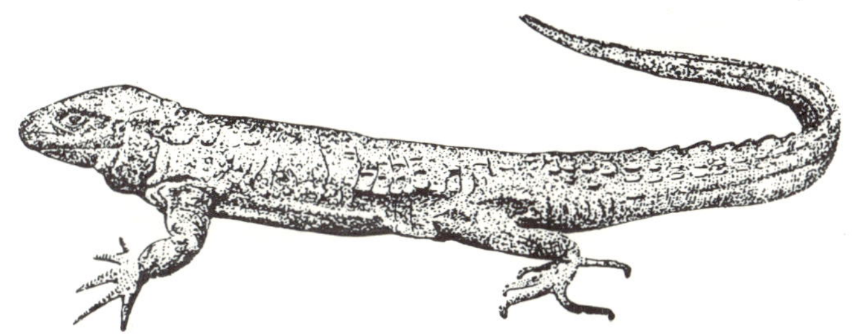

● SOUTH AMERICAN or GREAT TEGU
Tupinambis teguixin

Adult length 4 feet; dangerous when aroused.

Blunt head and long toes are distinctive markings.

These are powerful lizards and have a habit of raiding chicken farms. Usually found in the warmer areas of South America. They catch and kill chickens, break and eat the eggs. Often they fight with other lizards killing their opponents and eating them.

Can be tamed in captivity, but are unpredictable, often turning into mean creatures and chasing their keepers or attacking them.

● ALLIGATOR TEGU
Dracaena guyanensis

Average length 2 feet; largest 3 feet; somewhat dangerous.

Recognized by heavy jowled head and whip-like tail.

A South American lizard, noted for ability to travel fast and raid chicken farms. They can grasp and crush other creatures in their vise-like jaws. Have the strength to crush a man's hand.

Range: Tropical South America.

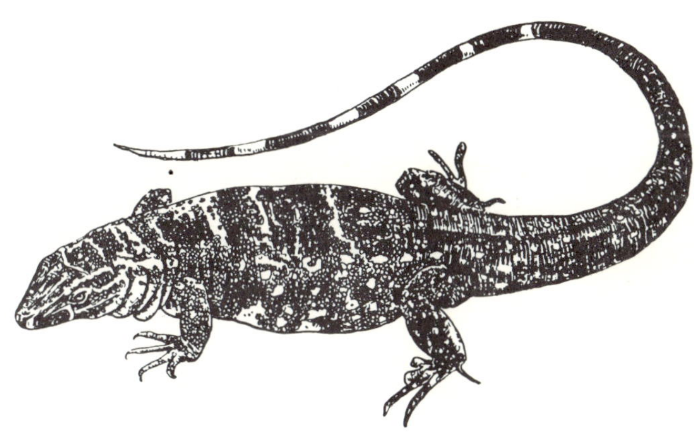

● TUATARA
Sphenodon punctatus

Average size 2 feet; largest 3 feet; harmless.

Dark olive-green.

Called the "Living Fossil" or "Ghost out of the Past", this creature has no family member living today. All other creatures of the order *Rhynchocephalia* are in museums as fossils.

They are sluggish and feed only upon insects. Are easy to capture because they have no good plan of defense or escape. Because of this the lizard-like reptiles are gradually being decimated. It is now protected by law and on the endangered species list.

Range: Only a few islands off New Zealand are known to be populated.

● BLACK TEGU
Tupinambis nigropunctatus

Average size 3 feet; largest 4 feet, 6 inches; dangerous; edible.

Black with yellow or white, crossing the back in bands.

A carnivorous, swift-running lizard of large size that is a terror in raiding chicken houses. Sometimes vicious—has been known to attack humans. Jaws are powerful enough to crush a hand, or kill a man by shaking and twisting if it gets a good hold. They are hunted for food in many parts of the world.

Range: Live in South America.

 # Peculiar Lizards 

● SAND LIZARD
Lacerta agilis

Average size 5 inches; largest 8 inches; harmless.

Brown or rusty above, sprinkled with light and dark spots. A dark, yellow-bordered band along the sides.

Common lizard of sandy areas on the European continent. Live on insects and spend most of their time scampering through grass and underbrush. This species lays eggs.

Range: Europe, from Russia to the Alps.

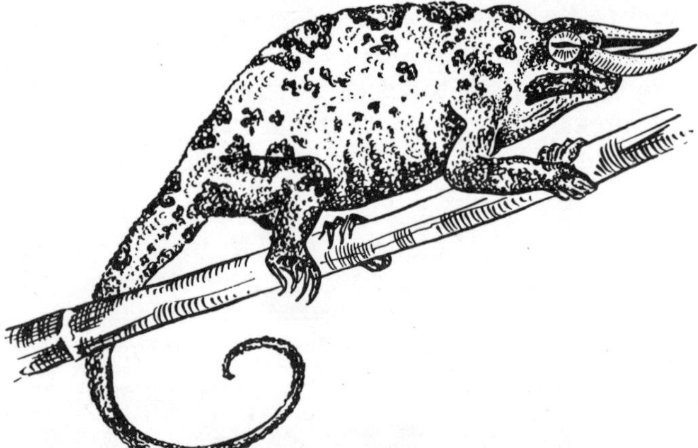

● THREE-HORNED CHAMELEON
Chameleo jacksoni

Average size 12 inches; largest 14 inches; harmless.

Distinguished by three horns on head.

Natives of East Africa believe this lizard to be poisonous and thus is feared and hated. Horns are coveted as ornaments by African women who string them on necklaces.

Range: Belgian Congo.

● WEST INDIAN CHAMELEON
Anolis sagrae

Average size 5 inches; largest 7 inches; harmless.

Usually a rich golden-brown with scattered dark blotches. Often pale longitudinal bands on the back.

Have adhesive pads like the Gecko and are quite agile, scampering around on the trees. They resemble in miniature an alligator, except the tail is flattened with a serrated edge on top. They change colors to every hue except green.

Range: Bahamas, Cuba and Jamaica.

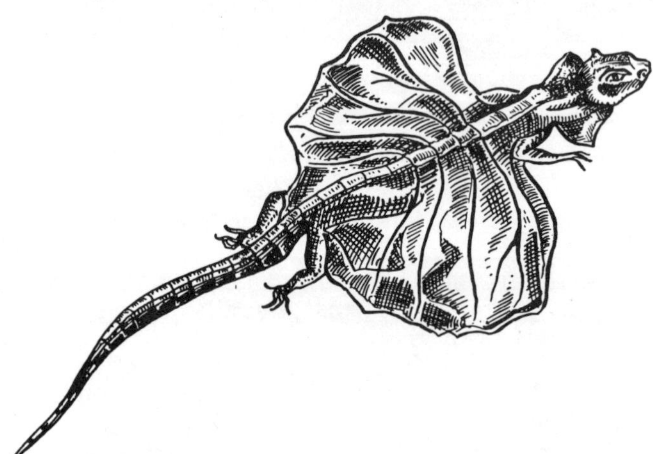

● FLYING DRAGON
Draco volans

Average size 9 inches; largest 12 inches; harmless.

Identified by wing spread (about 20 species, varying in size and color markings).

These lizards do not actually fly, but glide from the branches of trees to the ground when disturbed. Spend most of their time high in the trees, so are seldom seen by hunters. They devour all manner of insects.

Range: Native to Indo-Malayan region.

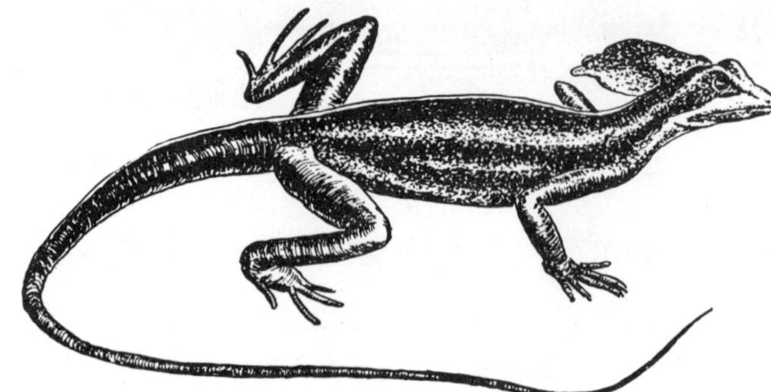

● BANDED BASILISK
Basiliscus vittatus

Average size 2 feet; largest 28 inches; harmless.

Identified by crown, resembling a weather vane on head; white lips and throat. Like a toad, is covered with fine scales. The hide will usually appear to be salt and pepper sprinkled.

This lizard is a fast and able runner, even on water! If startled, will take off for the nearest pond, skimming over the surface for several yards before diving to safety. Likes insects for food, preferring ants, flies and small worms.

Range: Mexico to Ecuador.

American Lizards

● OREGON ALLIGATOR LIZARD
Gerrhonotus multicarinatus scincicauda

Average size 8 inches; largest 11 inches; harmless.

Brownish or olive with 10 distinct crossbands. White spots on the outside margins of the crossbands.

Differs from other plated lizards, in that the tail is thicker and scales on the forward portion are quite rough; toward the end the scales get smooth. Have a tendency to bite when captured, although not capable of inflicting much of a wound. Will become quite tame in captivity.

Range: Washington, Oregon and California, west of the mountains.

speed when alarmed. This is done by running on hind feet alone, balancing with tail stretched out behind. At top speed they are so fast that one sees only a flash of movement.

Range: From Delaware to Florida and west to Nebraska.

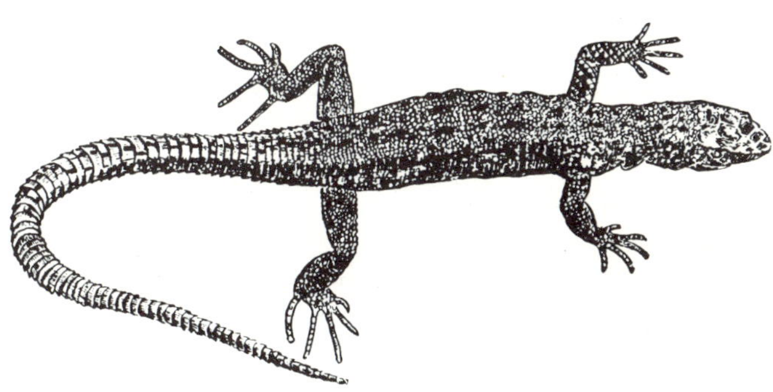

● ARIZONA NIGHT LIZARD
Xantusia arizonea

Average size 3½ inches; largest 5 inches; harmless.

Dark brown with fine black spots, long tail. A night roving lizard which dislikes sunlight. When the days are warm, this creature stays in the shade, usually under a rock or in a hollow log.

Feeds on insects and insect larvae.

Range: Found in Arizona only.

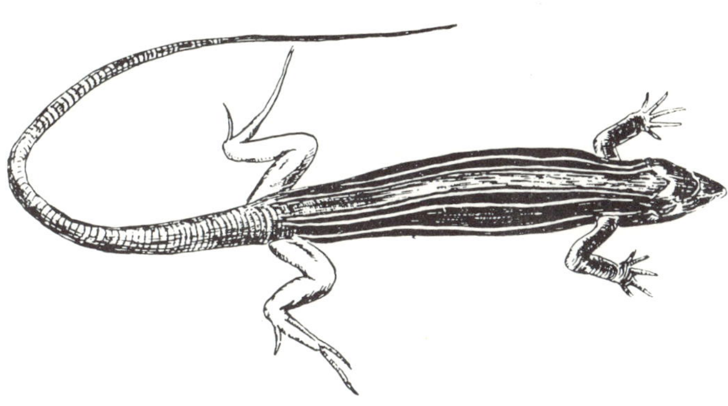

● SIX-LINED LIZARD
Cnemidophorus sexlineatus

Also called RACE-RUNNER.

Average size 8 inches; largest 10 inches; harmless.

Identified by six bright stripes down the back. Usually a broad, pale brownish band on middle of back from head to tail. Base color is usually brown, but they change shade continually.

A ground-preferring lizard, seldom seen climbing. Likes dry sandy soil and often observed on borders of dirt roads. Can travel at great rate of

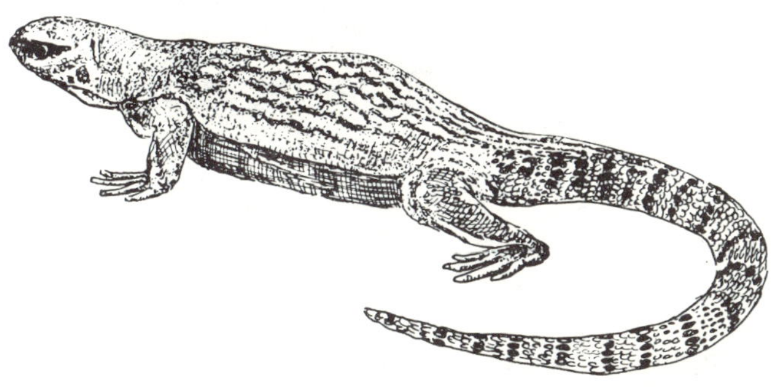

● DESERT IGUANA
Dipsosaurus d. dorsalis

Average size 10 inches; largest 15 inches; harmless; edible.

A row of enlarged scales down the middle of back identifies. Pale brown above with wavy longitudinal black lines. The lines enclose yellow spots. Grayish-white below.

A plant-eating lizard preferring leaves and flowers. Like other herbivorous lizards, is thick bodied and slow moving. Lives on sandy deserts and prefers plenty of hot sunshine.

Range: Southwestern states and Mexico.

American Lizards

● KING'S ALLIGATOR LIZARD *Gerrhonotus kingi*

Average size 12 inches; largest 17 inches; harmless.

Ground color, ashy-gray, or pale olive, crossed by bars of brown narrowly bordered with black. Tail is brightly barred and the head is mottled.

Apparently a night-roving lizard, for they are not often seen in daylight. Prefer some sunshine, but for the most part like shade and some dampness. Eat grasshoppers, beetles and bugs with hard shells mostly. Does not care for soft worms.

Range: New Mexico, Arizona and Northern Mexico.

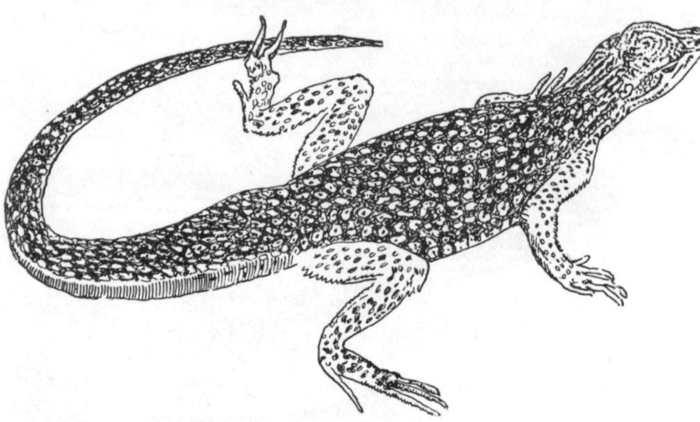

● FRINGE-TOED LIZARD *Uma notata*

Also called SAND LIZARD.

Average size 6 inches; largest 8½ inches; harmless.

Quite variable in body coloring, mostly conforming to the sandy ground the lizard travels on. Usually a brownish body with pale round blotches, borders touching. In center of each blotch is a black spot. Usually black spot on each side of abdomen.

A dry sand lizard with a habit of burrowing when disturbed. They feed on leaves, caterpillars, ants and bees.

Range: Desert country of Southern California, southwestern Arizona and the Colorado desert.

● SPOTTED LIZARD *Holbrookia maculata maculata*

Average size 4 inches; largest 5 inches; harmless.

Pale brown, yellowish or gray, with two rows of dark blotches on the back, kind of triangular; points directed toward the tail.

A very active lizard, capable of climbing and scampering over rocks and boulders. Usually are found on the ground. Eat insects, mostly beetles and grubs.

Range: Found in Texas, California and Arizona.

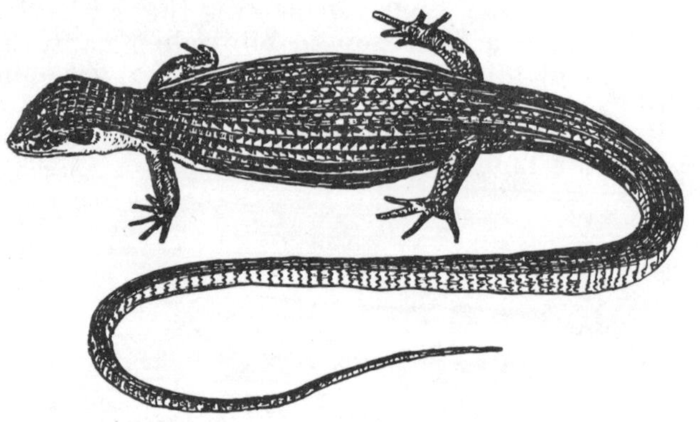

● CALIFORNIA ALLIGATOR LIZARD
Gerrhonotus coeruleus

Also called LONG-TAILED LIZARD.

Average size 12 inches; largest 16 inches; harmless.

Brown or olive with numerous dark spots and wavy crossbands. Many of these bordered with white spots. Soft strips of skin on the sides have patches of white. Belly greenish-white.

A forest and mountain lizard, doing well at elevations from 7,000 to 9,000 feet. Because of their size, are not as agile as the Swifts and some other smaller lizards. Feed on insects, mostly grubs and slow-crawling worms. Sometimes they capture other smaller lizards. Can cast off the tail without being touched.

Range: Found only in the coastal regions of northern California.

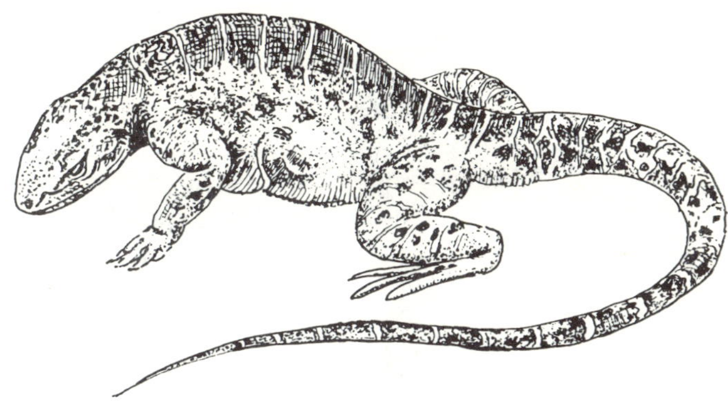

● TEXAS ALLIGATOR LIZARD

Gerrhonotus liocephalus

Also called LONG-TAILED PLATED LIZARD. Average size 10 inches; largest 12 inches; harmless.

Brownish with irregular and obscure dark and light hues.

There are several species of this lizard in the Southwest, which may be recognized by slender shape and rather large head. Limbs are small and tail long and brittle.

They have a habit of parting with their tails easily and seldom are captive lizards found with perfect tails.

They live well in captivity if in a warm and dry spot.

Texas to California is general range.

● LEOPARD LIZARD

Crotaphytes wislizeni

Average size 10 inches; largest 12 inches; harmless.

Yellowish-brown above, covered with black blotches and red spots. Yellowish bands on back and tail. Lower surface is creamy-white.

This lizard does not like stony areas such as the Collared Lizard prefers. Usually found in the hottest and driest of sandy wastes.

Is very aggressive, often attacking and devouring other lizards larger than itself as well as small snakes.

Range: Southern Utah, Nevada, Arizona and Southern California.

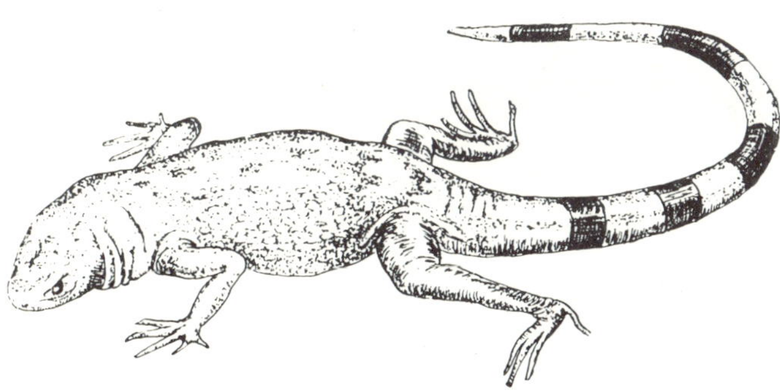

● ZEBRA-TAILED LIZARD

Callisaurus draconoides

Average size 5 inches; largest 6½ inches; harmless.

Grayish, dotted with white; two rows of angular or V-shaped blotches on back. Angular bands on the tail. Belly white. Lower surface of tail white with black bars.

A small lizard with flattened head and long legs. Is an extremely fast runner and can skim over the desert sands almost faster than the eye can follow. Sometimes running on hind feet alone with tail curled up. Eats insects and small blossoms.

Abundant in desert regions of United States.

● COLLARED LIZARD

Crotaphytus collaris

Average size 10 inches; largest 12 inches.

Distinguished by two dark bands across the back of neck and three black dots parallel on the sides.

A warm climate lizard, living more eastward than the Horned Lizard. Preferring underbrush occasionally. One of the largest of American lizards.

Range: Central and Western United States.

Long Tailed Lizards

● GREEN LIZARD
Lacerta viridis

Average length 1 foot; largest 14 inches; harmless.

Solid green over all; light yellow spot on head; some streaked or spotted with yellow.

A European lizard, common in France. Quite friendly and harmless. Can be taught to eat out of hand quickly. Gypsies have a ritual of placing this lizard in a tiny casket and having the oldest man in the tribe pass it among the families. Each Gypsy spits in the casket. This dispels all illness for the next year. The casket is thrown in running water. Anyone who finds and opens "The Thing" will be visited by all the maladies thus thrown off.

Range: Central Europe.

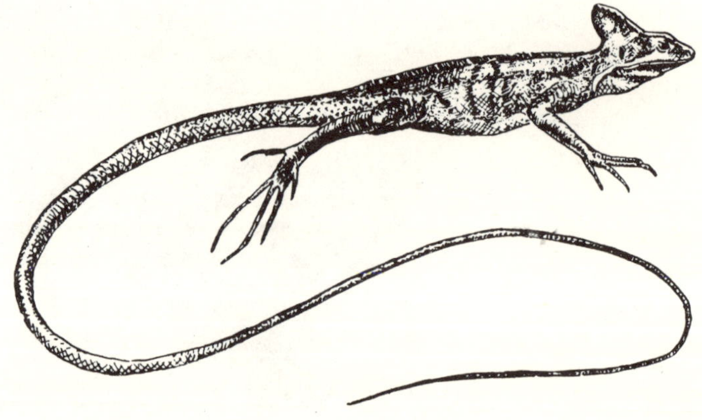

● CONE-HEADED LIZARD
Laemanctus serratus

Average size 2 feet; largest 3 feet; harmless. Identified by extremely long tail and top-knot on the head.

A tree-roving lizard, feeding on insects. Member of the Basilisk tribe, very agile and hard to see or capture. They can dart away with blinding speed, either in tree limbs or on the ground. Feed on flower petals as well as insects they capture.

Range: Mexico to Ecuador.

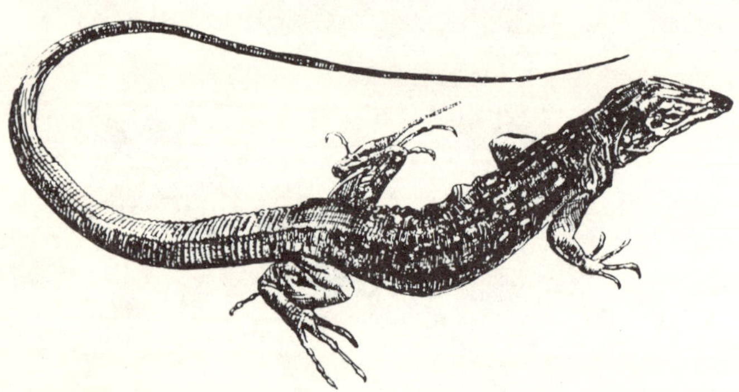

● WHIP-TAILED LIZARD
Cnemidophorous bocourti

Average size 10 inches; largest 14 inches; harmless.

Dark brown and sandy colored with bony ridges showing on the back and square plate-like scales on the sides. Tail has number of serrations like rings. Yellowish dots on the back.

Member of the Race Runner family, which gets its name from lurking along the edge of sandy roads as if inviting a race with passing pedestrians. They eat insects and small worms. Are very fast and strictly a ground lizard.

Range: Mexico.

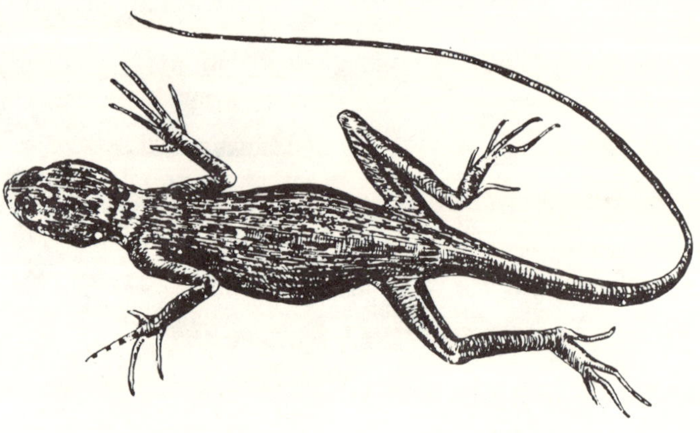

● TREE-RUNNER
Uraniscodon plica

Average size 12 inches; largest 16 inches; harmless.

Scales are very minute, with a row of enlarged scales on the back. Long slender tail and very long hind legs. Olive-gray above, spotted with rusty-brown. There is a dark collar.

This is a lizard which haunts old buildings and tree trunks. They lie in wait for insects, hanging with head down. When a passing beetle or grasshopper comes in sight, they dart with lightning speed.

Range: South America, Trinidad and the island of Granada.

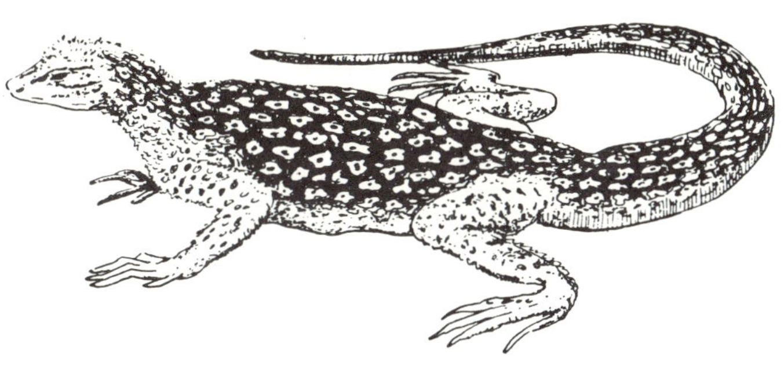

● SAND LIZARD *Acanthodactylus boskianus*

Average size 7 inches; largest 10 inches; harmless.

Spots of golden-yellow with traces of rusty-red inside. Basic color is palid according to ground the lizard moves on.

A Spanish type of Sand Lizard with fringed toes that allows the fast movement over desert sands. Feeds on insects.

Found in Spain and the desert portions of Africa and Arabia.

● SPINY LIZARD *Zonorous ciganteus*

Average size 12 inches; largest 16 inches; harmless.

Identified by a thick set of spines throughout the body and tail.

Don't step on this desert lizard. Its covering of sharp spines would be painful. They like scampering in the hot sun and sand, retiring with the cool of the night.

Feed on insects, which they catch on the tip of the tongue.

Range: South Africa.

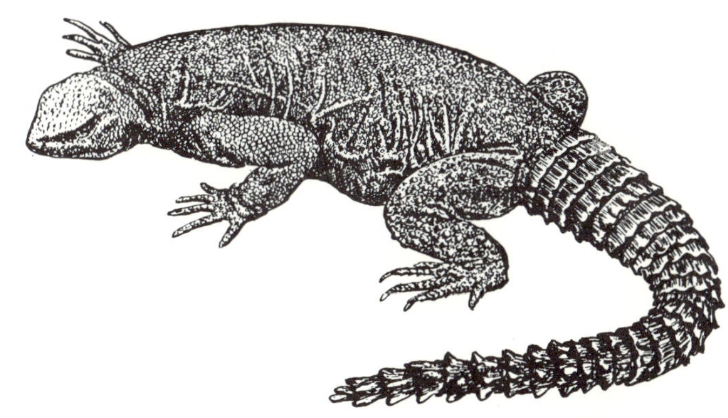

● CURL-TAIL LIZARD *Liocephalus carinatus*

Average size 10 inches; largest 12 inches; harmless.

Body covered with coarse bristling scales; thin tail curls above body.

A very active lizard, living both in the trees and on the ground. They feed mostly on insects, which they catch with ease. Prefer warm climate and enjoy considerable sunlight.

Common in Cuba and found throughout the West Indies; has been introduced into South Florida.

● SPINY TAILED MASTIGURE *Uromastyx spinipes*

Average size 14 inches; largest 20 inches; harmless; edible.

Identified by heavy spines on tail and smooth scales on body and head.

Usually spend nights and cool days burrowed in the sand, coming out when the sun is shining and the weather warm. Difficult to catch. Once burrowed in, they are almost impossible to pull out. Arabs hunt them steadily for food.

Range: Sahara Desert, Africa.

Chameleons

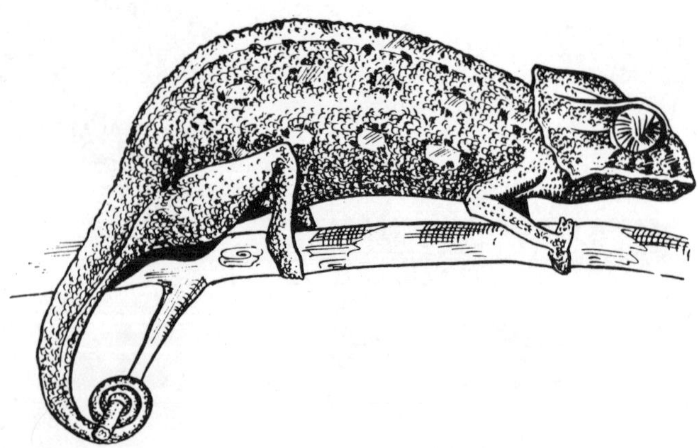

● **CHAMELEON** *Chameleo vulgaris*

Average size 5 inches; largest 9 inches; harmless.
These Old World lizards are the true chameleons.
Aside from their ability to change color, they bear
little resemblance to the so-called chameleons of this
continent—or indeed to any other lizards. The head
is topped by a hood or helmet-like structure. The
sticky, hollow tongue, as long as the body, is a highly
effective insect catching machine. Bulging eyes move
independently of each other. The tail, like a monkey's,
can be rolled up or used to swing from a tree limb.
They are tree dwellers and almost helpless on the
ground.

There is a giant chameleon in Madagascar that
grows to 3 feet. Another species, native to East
Africa, called Jackson's Chameleon, has a bony horn
pointing straight from the nose and two horns between the eyes.

Range: Mediterranean countries, Africa and
India.

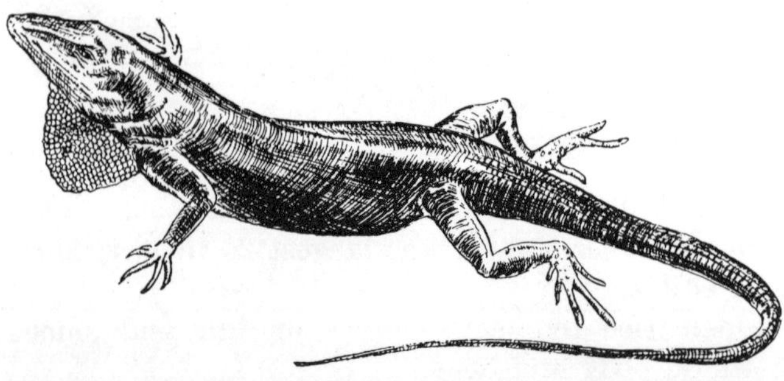

● **GREEN ANOLE** *Anolis carolinesis*

Known as the AMERICAN CHAMELEON.
Average size 6 inches; largest 7½ inches; harmless. Over 300 known species of anole are found in
tropical America but only 4 in the U. S.

There are actually no chameleons in North
America. The anoles, like the true chameleons, can
change color according to temperature or other
physiological conditions. Colors range from green
to rust to brown. The male, in either an agressive
or love-making mood brings on a show of his brilliant
red throat fan.

These little creatures are the "chameleons"
usually sold in the pet stores. They make delightful
pets, apparently enjoying human companionship.
They can be trained to take food—preferably live
insects—from one's fingers. They will lap water from
drops on foliage but not from a dish.
They are daylight animals, sleep at night.

Range: Carolinas to Florida and west to Texas.
They may range northward, but it depends on the
severity of the winters.

● **GIANT ANOLE** *Anolis equestris*

Also called the CUBAN CHAMELEON.

Average size 12 inches; largest 16 inches;
harmless.
Identified by the large pouch in lower jaw, big
head and long tail. Has a ridge of fin-like soft horns
down the back which stands up when aroused. The
color varies from brown to yellow and sometimes a
brilliant green.
Essentially a West Indian anole. The largest come
from Cuba. They live in trees and have great agility
in leaping from branch to branch.

Range: Mexico, Central America and West
Indies. Particularly plentiful in Jamaica and Cuba.
A subspecies called the Knight Anole is found in
Dade County, Florida. This anole is easily distin-
guished from any other in the U. S. because of its
super-size and the tubercles on the head.

Spiny Tailed Swifts

● **COLLARED SWIFT**   *Sceloporus torquatus*

Also called PORCUPINE LIZARD.

Average size 10 inches; largest 12 inches; harmless.

Greenish-gray above, with broad black, yellow-bordered collar.

This is the largest of the Swifts. of which there are 20 sub species. They like very hot desert surroundings and hide in the sand when the sun goes down.

Home of this one is Mexico.

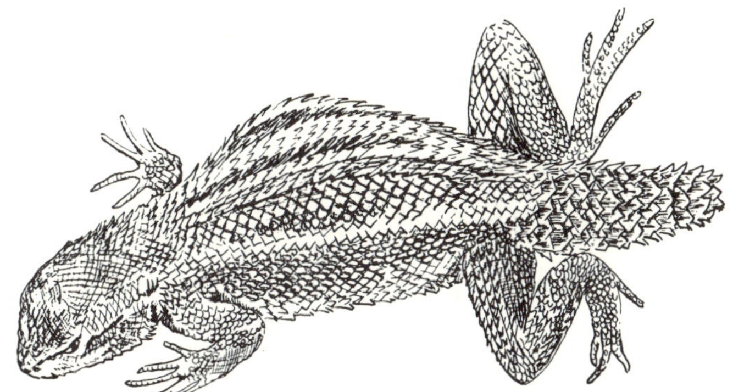

● **SOUTHERN PRAIRIE LIZARD**

Sceloporous undulatus consobrinus

Also called YELLOW-STRIPED SWIFT.

Average size 5 inches; largest 6 inches; harmless.

Greenish-yellow. On each side of back are two distinct stripes of yellow. On back there are less distinct but wider bands.

Lives mostly in arid regions of the southwest and can find good footing on rocks as well as sand. Travels fast when pursued.

Prefer warm and dry atmosphere and living quarters.

This species occurs in all parts of Texas, northward to the Dakotas and west to California.

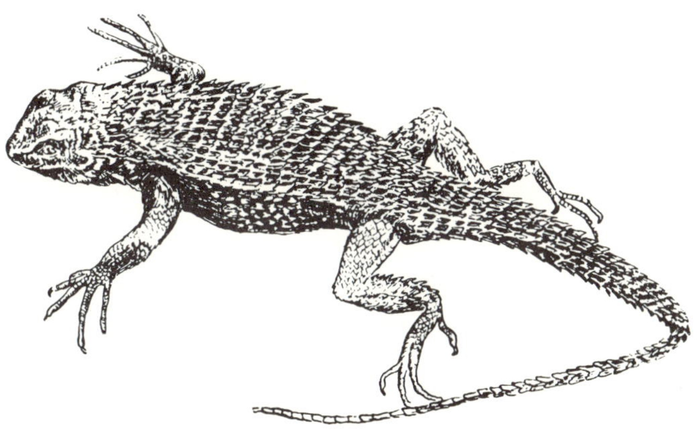

● **TEXAS SPINY SWIFT**   *Sceloporous olivaceus*

Average size 9 inches; largest 10½ inches; harmless.

Dull olive, sometimes greenish; series of narrow wavy crossbands on back, with a ring-like formation at tail.

Living for the most part on trunks of trees, or fallen logs over which they can run with astonishing speed. Often they will burrow in the ground at the foot of a tree, usually in the evening.

Abundant from Texas to Mexico and eastward to Florida.

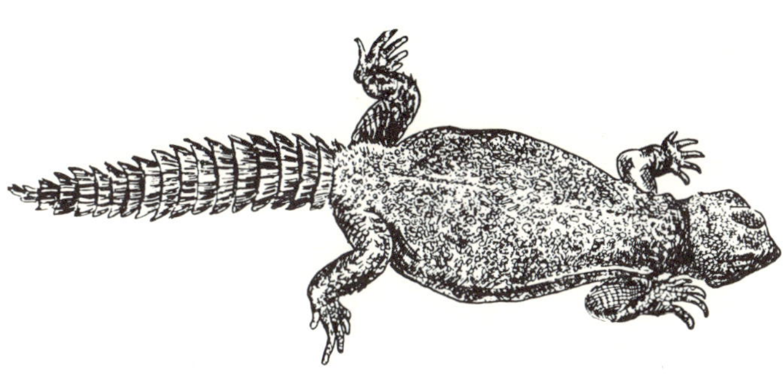

● **SPINY-TAILED LIZARD**

Uromastyx acanthinur

Average size 14 inches; largest 18 inches; harmless.

Distinguished by a small blunt head, with tiny bead-like eyes. Curious tail like a spiked war club. Usually dull brown or yellow.

These lizards inhabit the desert regions and prefer a very hot and dry atmosphere. They need water, but do not drink, absorbing the fluid through their skin when condensation such as dew strikes them. When attempt is made to capture them, the tail is used as a club, vigorously swishing from right to left.

Range: Deserts of North Africa.

Swifts

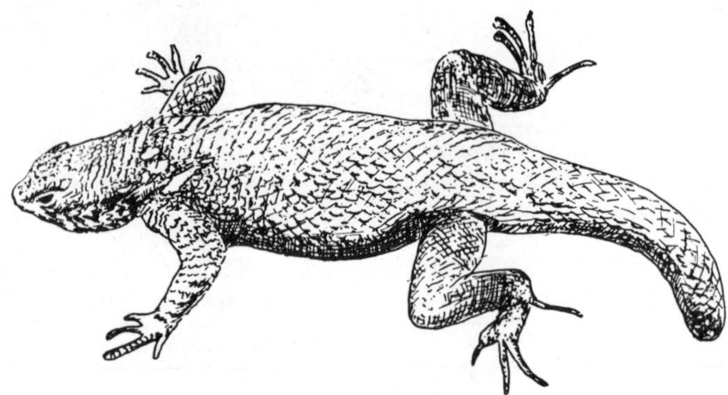

● SONORA SPINY LIZARD

Sceloporus clarki

Average size 8 inches; largest 10 inches; harmless.

Mostly uniform dull gray. They have the power to cause a bright green spot to appear in the center of each spiny scale which makes it look like a bit of tree stalk or bush.

When approached they can dash away with lightning speed. Like it hot and spend the day chasing around catching insects. Crawl under the sand at night.

Found in the arid regions of Arizona, New Mexico and Texas.

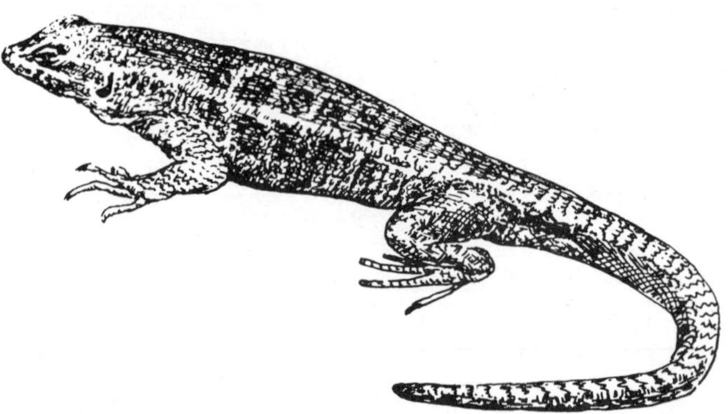

● WESTERN FENCE LIZARD

Sceloporous occidentalis

Average length 5 inches; largest 8 inches; harmless.

Dark green above. Two light bands across the body, separated by 18 rows of scales. Back has irregular spots.

In this type the scales are all keeled, terminating in points which are needle-sharp. Appear to bristle all over, like spines. They are seen in woodland, scampering over logs and on rail fences.

Range: Central California to Washington.

● EASTERN FENCE LIZARD

Sceloporous undulatus

Also called UNDULATED LIZARD.

Average size 6 inches; largest 12 inches; edible.

Identified by the crest on top of head and back, which is short, thick, with strongly keeled scales.

Abounds in pine forests, usually spending most time in the bark of trees as a resting place. Feeds on insects, such as in decayed wood.

Found throughout the Western States of North America.

● SIDE BLOTCHED LIZARD

Uta stansburiana

Average size, 5 inches; largest, 6 inches; harmless.

Bluish-drab with numerous small whitish dots. There are no dark blotches on the back. A dark spot behind the fore limb.

A terrestrial lizard, living among the rocks and sub-arid regions. Very agile. Have the habit of running on hind legs when pursued. Feet have adhesive discs, claws are strong. Eat mealworms and grasshoppers.

Range: Utah, Nevada, Idaho and Southern California.

Poisonous and Horned Lizards 

● GILA MONSTER
Heloderma suspectum

Average size 18 inches; largest 24 inches; poisonous.

Mottled pink and black; has beadlike tubercles rather than scales.

Terror of the western desert country, the Gila Monster is given a wide berth by all who know it. The bite, quickly poisonous to animals, is fatal to man in some cases. Should be treated as a snake bite. Can grasp and hang onto an object with the tenacity of a bulldog.

They are quite agile and hiss like a snake when cornered.

Range: Arizona and Sonora, Mexico.

● MEXICAN BEADED LIZARD
Heloderma horridum

Average size 14 inches; largest 27 inches; poisonous.

Pale yellow and black, the black predominating. Head is entirely black. Tail long. Back covered with yellow blotches. Five yellow rings encircle the tail.

Brother to the Gila Monster of the North American deserts, this poisonous lizard is the tropical version. There are only two poisonous lizards.

It is believed the Bearded Lizards live mostly on snake eggs dug from the sand, although their flat tongue, darting out to great length is suitable for picking up ants. They will attack small mammals, or anything they can catch.

Range: Mexico to Central America.

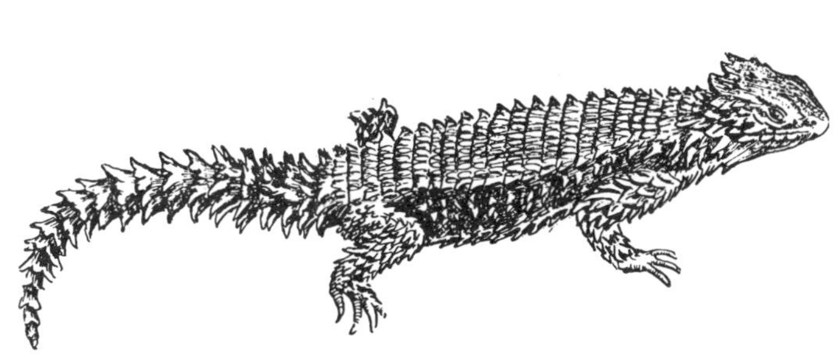

● GIANT ZONURE
Zonurus giganteus

Average size 18 inches; largest 24 inches; harmless.

Identified by the large spines, sprouting from entire body.

A lizard of the dry, rocky areas, going underground at night and during the times of hibernation. A wild sort of lizard, which is never seen tame in captivity. Feeds mostly on earthworms.

Range: South Africa.

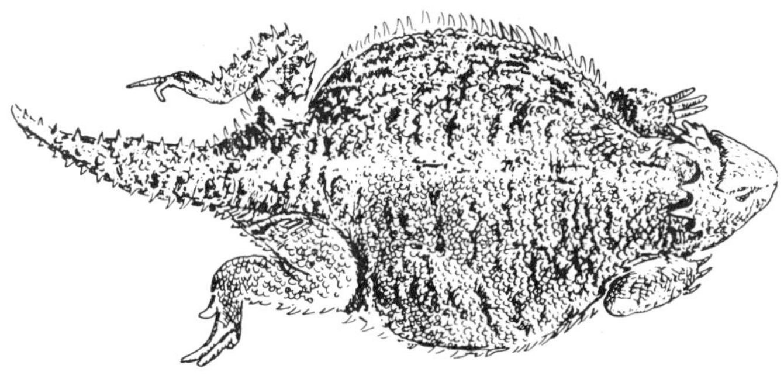

● MEXICAN HORNED LIZARD
Phrynosoma orbiculare

Average size 3½ inches; largest 5 inches; harmless.

Dull brick-red. Horns are quite flat and but slightly developed, less than other species of this genus.

Of all the members of the Horned Lizard family, characterized by the ability to squirt blood from their eyes, this particular one is most adept at it. Ditmar reported that a jet of blood as fine as a hair shot out five feet against the wall when it was being handled. Live in the hot desert sand.

Range: Desert regions of Mexico.

Horned Lizards

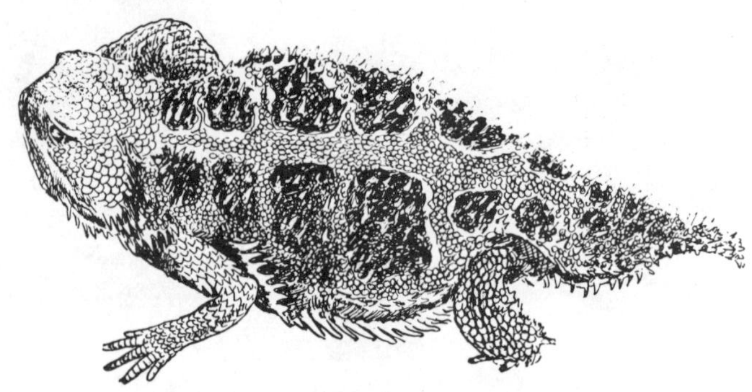

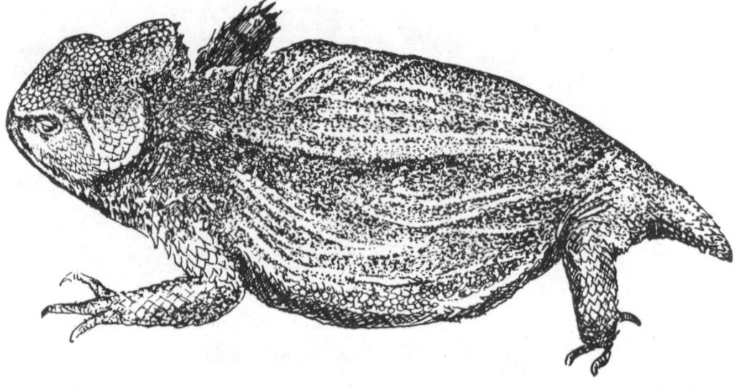

● PYGMY HORNED LIZARD

Phrynosoma d. douglassi

Average length 4 inches; largest 5 inches; harmless.

Quite often they are pink with white spots, but will be the same background color, as a rule.

Small in size with short limbs, very blunt snout and small horns. They are not common anywhere. (Prefer rocky ground).

Range: Southwest United States.

● DITMARS' HORNED LIZARD

Phrynosoma ditmarsi

Average size 4 inches; largest 4 inches; harmless.

Sandy-red with obscure crossbands on back.

So far as known only one living specimen has been observed. This by Raymond L. Ditmars, curator of reptiles at New York Zoo. Only two specimens have been seen. Both were taken in Mexico. The living specimen kept at New York Zoo for a year, was quite healthy and energetic, living on insects.

Ditmars believed the smooth skin might account for the fact that snakes make off with most of the lizards of this species.

Range: Mexico.

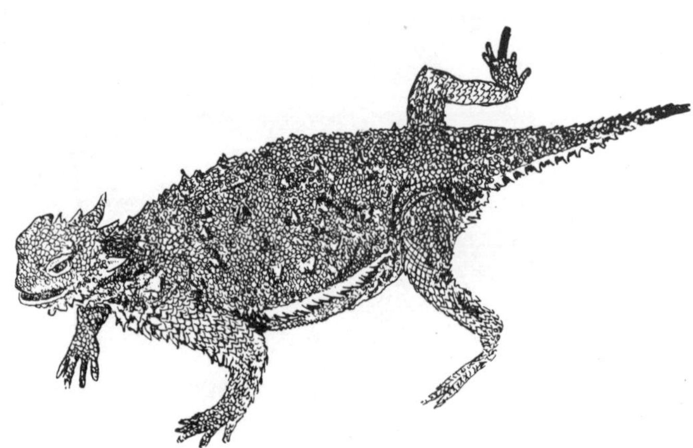

● SAN DIEGO HORNED LIZARD

Phynosoma c. blainvillei

Average length 6 inches; largest 8 inches; harmless.

Combination of sprinkled yellow, gray and black to match the desert sand. Identified by the horns.

Seen on the arid and desert sands of Texas and western states. Sometimes taken by tourists as souvenirs. They have a habit of puffing up when angry so their eyes bulge and two tiny streams of blood squirt from them.

The Texas Lizard is brownish or reddish.

Range: Western, central and southern United States.

● DESERT HORNED LIZARD

Phrynosoma platyrhinos

Average size 4½ inches; largest 5½ inches; harmless.

Body appears smooth with rows of enlarged scales on each side of chin, pinkish-gray. Large dark patch on each side of the nape. Belly very white.

An abundant species throughout the Pacific states from Washington to Utah.

American Horned Lizards

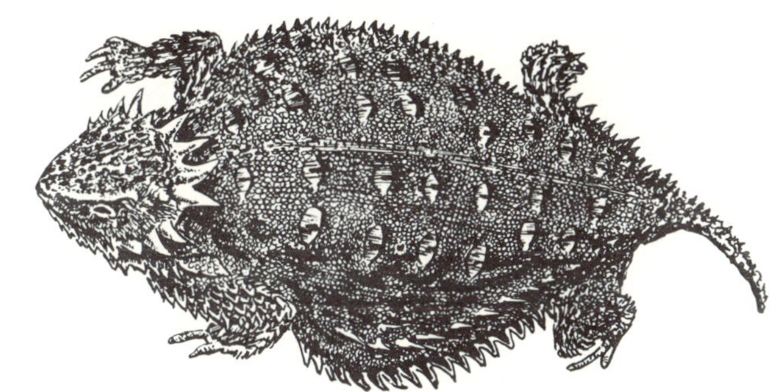

● SALT LAKE HORNED LIZARD
Phrynosoma d. ornatum

Also called ORNATE HORNED LIZARD.

Average size 4 inches; largest 6 inches; harmless.

Distinguished by short legs. A series of dark blotches along the back from head to tail. Usually about ten, in two rows. Short stubby tail.

A desert lizard, which is more on the order of a toad. Feeds like a toad, by flicking a long tongue and catching an insect on the end. They prefer the blazing sun and will burrow in the sand long before the sun has set. Are quite fast in scampering on the hot sand.

Range: Idaho, Nevada, Utah.

● REGAL HORNED LIZARD
Phynosoma solare

Average size 5¼ inches; largest 6 inches; harmless.

Pale brown with a narrow band on back. Two dark blotches on the neck and three or four on each side. Color is yellowish-white beneath.

This is one of the most imposing of the Horned Lizards. The continuous row of flat spines upon the head, give the effect of a crown. They are in perfect alignment. Considered a rare species, although those who penetrate the deserts say they are common and a true desert type.

Range: The Gila and Colorado deserts; Lower California and Sonora, Mexico.

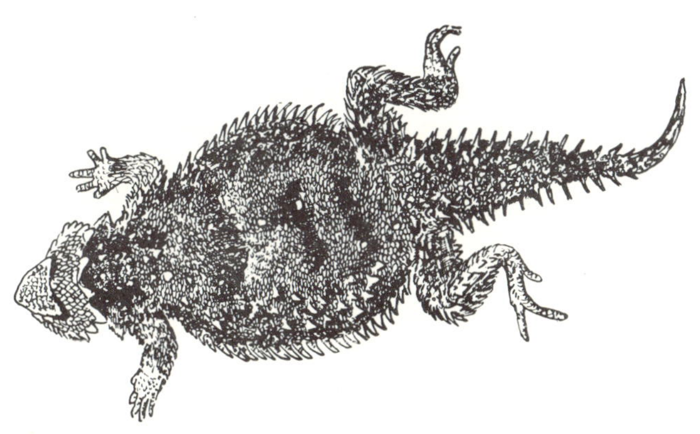

● MOUNTAIN SHORT-HORNED LIZARD
Phrynosoma douglassii hernandesi

Average size 4 inches; largest 5½ inches; harmless.

Identified by a corona of spines about the head. Two rows of spines down the back. Fairly heavy-set tail, thickly spined.

An abundant form of Horned Lizard of the plains area. Have the ability to match almost exactly the ground on which they travel. Sometimes they are black when on black lava areas; again pink with whitish dots when in pinkish soil.

Range: Great Plains and Rocky Mountain area of western United States.

● TEXAS HORNED LIZARD
Phrynosoma cornutum

Average size 4½ inches; largest 6 inches; harmless.

Broad body with small tail. Strongly defined yellow band on back extends from head down to the tail. On each side of the nape is a large dark blotch. Three dark round spots on each side of back are bordered in the rear with a crescent of yellow. Belly yellow with numerous dark round spots.

Most abundant of the Horned Toads of the West, although carrying the name "Texas", is not actually appropriate. This is the Horned Toad brought back East by travelers in the West.

Range: Throughout the Western States, most abundant in Texas.

Skinks

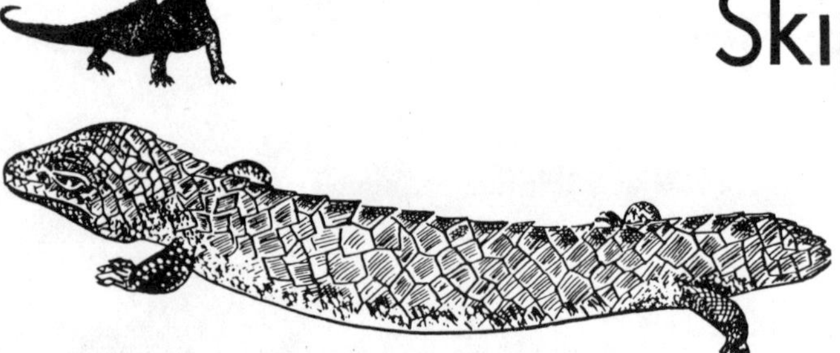

● **STUMP-TAILED SKINK**   *Trachydosaurus rugosus*

Average size 6 inches; largest 10; harmless. Distinguished by tail which almost resembles another head. Brown, spotted or banded with yellow.

Spends most of life digging in the sand, or lying in the sun on a stone; feeds on worms and small snakes. Does well in captivity and eats most anything. Range: Australia.

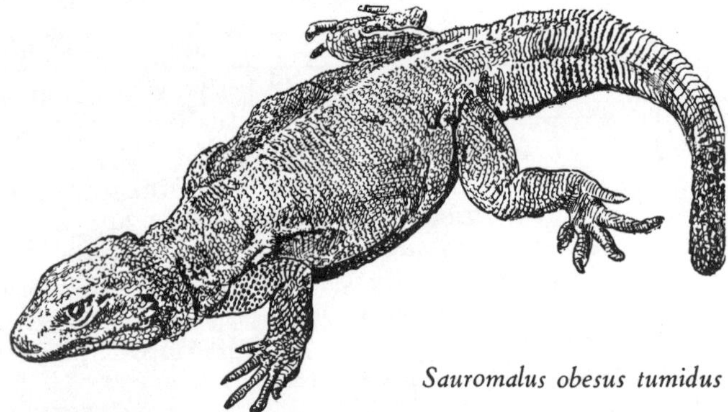

Sauromalus obesus tumidus

● **ARIZONA CHUCKWALLA**

Average size 12 inches; largest 18 inches; harmless. Uniform rusty-brown. Young are banded or marbled.

A fat-bodied lizard with stumpy tail. Slow moving and unable to show much speed when threatened. Food is mostly flowers and tender leaves.

Like an extremely high temperature and cannot endure coolness of any degree. They wither and die when temperature goes below the high 80's. Can survive in heat that would be unbearable for other animals.

Range: Deserts of Arizona and New Mexico.

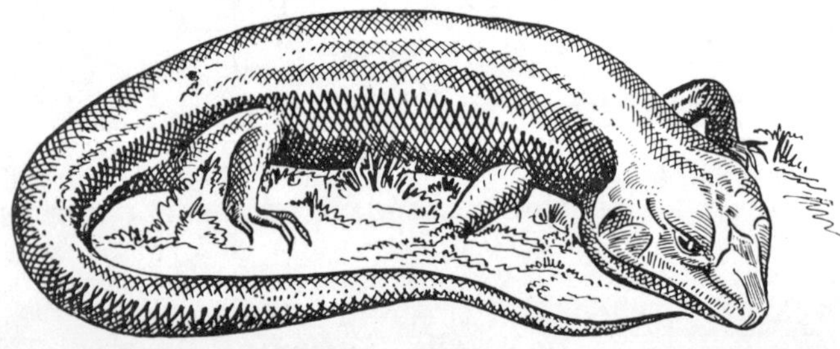

● **GREAT PLAINS SKINK**   *Eumeces oboletus*

Average size 11 inches; largest 14; harmless. Large head, well developed legs, smooth scales.

Timid and easily frightened, they scamper off when disturbed. Usually burrow in top soil or under leaves. Range: Throughout central United States and northern Mexico.

● **FLORIDA KEYS MOLE SKINK**

Eumeces e. egregius

Average size 3 inches; largest 4; harmless. Olive to reddish-brown. Four equally distant white stripes. Two on each side of the body and traversing the centers of single rows of scales. Stripes are margined.

The smallest and most snake-like of the Skinks in the United States. Body is so round it is almost worm-like. Legs are small and weak. Feeds on small insects and worms.

Range: South Florida and the Keys.

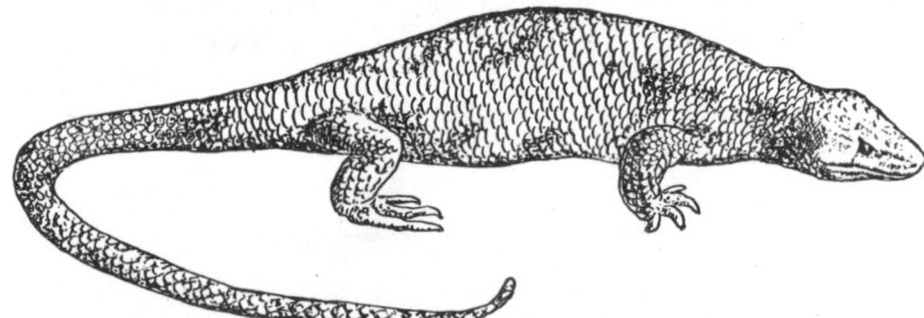

● **MONKEY-TAILED SKINK**   *Corucia zebrata*

Average length 8 inches; largest 12 inches; harmless. Brownish, shading to yellow. Long tail.

A tree-living Skink of the Pacific islands. Feeds on fruits and nuts as well as insects. Natives eat them. Range: Only on the Solomon Islands.

Scincus officinalis

● **DESERT SKINK**
Also called EGYPTIAN SKINK.

Average size 6 inches; largest 8 inches; harmless. Cream color, crossed by blackish or dark red bands.

Has a nose like a scoop and feathery appendages from toes. Lives in the desert and prefers temperature above 90°. Range: North Africa.

Skinks

● GIANT SKINK *Tiliqua gigas*

Average size 12 inches; largest 2 feet; harmless.

Slaty-gray crossed by dark bands; covered with large, smooth scales of a satiny luster. Tail is quite short.

Largest of the skinks and more like the lizards than snakes, although, as in all the breed, legs are quite short. This member of the family is a meat eater and captures small birds and large insects as a steady diet. Raids nests whenever possible.

Range: Guinea and Java.

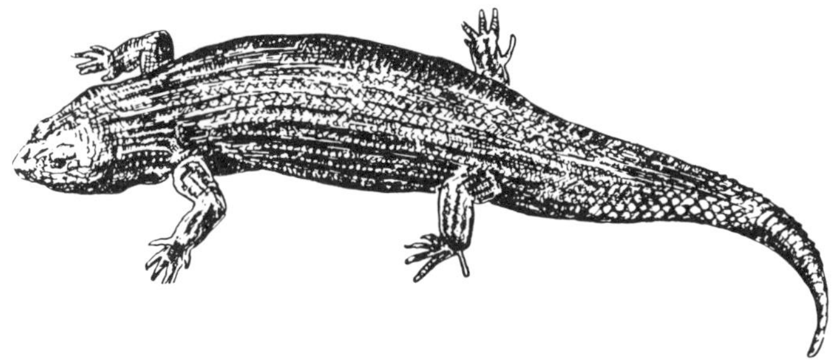

● CUNNINGHAM'S SKINK *Egernia cunninghami*

Average size 4 inches; largest 7 inches; harmless.

Fat, round-bodied, ground color of dark brown. Fine lines or vague serration from head to tail on back. Thick head and beady eyes; short tail.

A sand-loving, short-legged lizard of the land down under. Spends the days rooting about for worms and insects buried out of sight in the leaves and grass, or between rocks. Enjoys a comparatively high temperature. Range: Australia.

● WESTERN SKINK *Eumeces skiltonianus*

Average size 5 inches; largest 7 inches; harmless.

Olive color, with two whitish lines on each side, embracing a dark band. Upper stripes are bordered by a black band.

Smooth and shiny, almost snake-like in appearance. Has short limbs. Can travel quite fast, using a serpent-like motion.

Range: Washington, Oregon, California.

● FIVE-LINED SKINK *Eumeces fasciatus*

Also called NORTHERN BLUE - TAILED SKINK; RED-HEADED LIZARD; SCORPION.

Average length 7 inches; largest on record 10 inches; harmless.

Young are jet black with five bright yellow stripes. Tail is brilliant blue. Older males have brownish tinge which becomes fiery red.

Believed to be poisonous by many persons, although this is not so.

Range: Eastern United States from Massachusetts to Florida and as far west as Texas. Most plentiful in Southeast.

Common in pine tree forests.

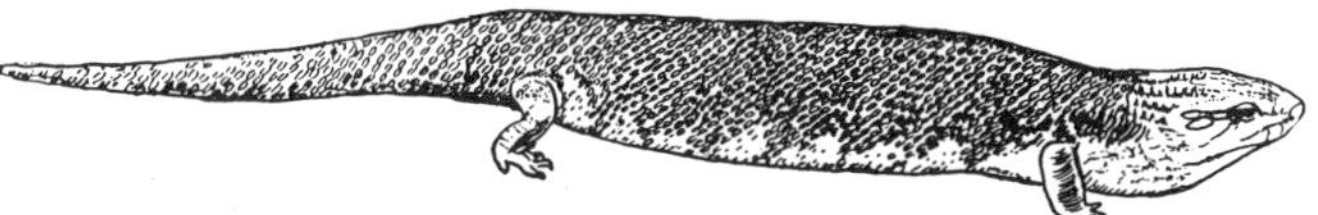

● GIANT SKINK *Tiliqua scincoides*

Also called BLUE-TONGUED SKINK.

Average size 14 inches; largest 24 inches; harmless.

Smooth, shiny and flattened body. Yellowish-brown above, with dark transverse bands. Has a deep purple tongue.

This is the largest member of the Skink family. Thrive on both fruit and meat. They like earthworms and will eat bananas or other fruit of like nature.   Range: Native to Australia.

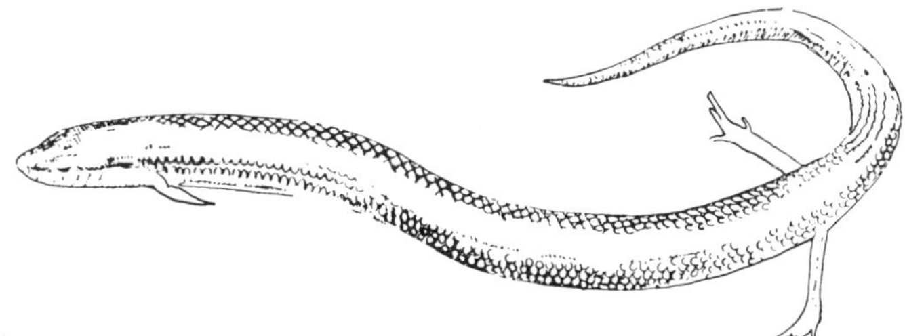

● SAND SKINK *Chalcides sepsiodes*

Average size 6 inches; largest 8 inches; harmless.

Clothed in smooth shining scales, conical snout. Has four very small limbs, which are seldom used.

Another snake-like lizard, living in the sand. All the qualities of a lizard are present, including the limbs, yet the movements and appearance is that of a snake. When disturbed they can disappear in the sand in a swimming motion, faster than a lizard. While carrying the name of "Skink," this is a lowly member of that family.

Range: Found in the reddish sands of the Sahara Desert and Arabia.

● FRINGED GECKO   *Uroplatus fimbriatus*

Also called BARK GECKO.

Average size 5 inches; largest 7 inches: harmless.

Identified by flat paddle-like tail and skin resembling the bark of a tree. Has large eyes and vertical pupils.

A tree-dwelling lizard with adhesion pads on the toes which are so powerful it is almost impossible to pull them loose, once they are attached. When lying flat on a tree trunk, it takes a sharp eye to distinguish the creature.

Range: Madagascar.

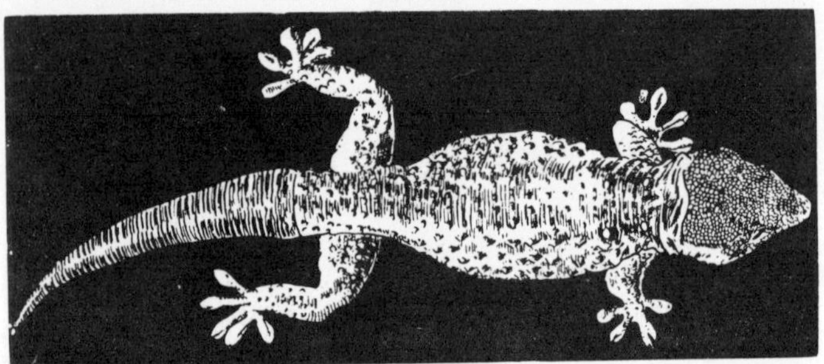

● WHITE-SPOTTED GECKO   *Tarentola amnularis*

Average size 4 inches; largest 6 inches; harmless.

Pale gray, sometmes pinkish with dark bands crossing the back. On the forward portion of the body are four white spots. The back is studded with small tubercles.

This lizard has enormous adhesive power in the pads of its feet. Can adhere to anything, even a pane of glass. They eat insects which are captured by scampering over rocks and tree trunks, often in inverted position.

Range: Abyssinia, Egypt and Arabia.

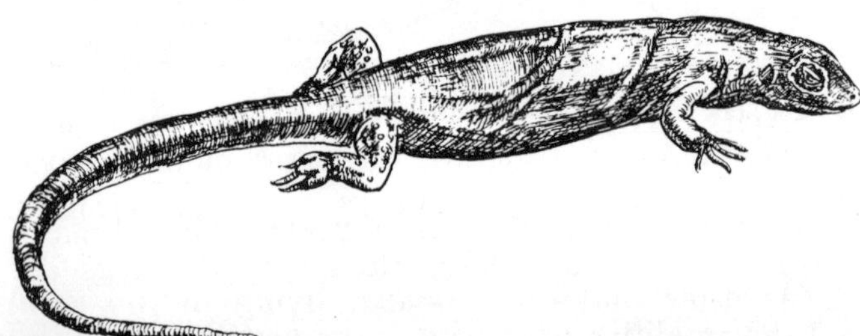

● REEF GECKO   *Sphaerodactylus notatus*

Average size 2 inches; largest 2⅝ inches; harmless.

Brownish-yellow with scattered spots of reddish-brown. Central dark marking on the head, becoming broader in the rear. The scales are keeled.

This is a small and secretive lizard, which apparently has traveled in ship's cargoes to be transplanted in a new home. Seen about rain water cisterns and under planks on the docks.

Range: Key West Islands of Florida, the Bahamas and Cuba.

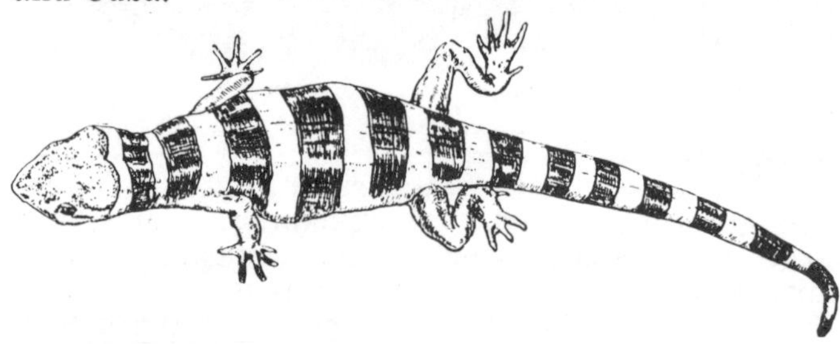

● BANDED GECKO   *Coleonyx variegatus*

Average size 3 inches; largest 4 inches; harmless.

Two forms are observed—banded and spotted. The banded is ground yellow crossed by bands of chestnut brown. The bands terminate on the sides except at the tail, which they encircle. The spotted form is yellow with irregular brown blotches. Eyelids are bordered in yellow.

Mostly nocturnal and can be seen coming out from under stone crevices at sundown. Not as fast as Swifts and other lizards. Are sluggish until captive, then will do all in their power to bite the the fingers that hold them.

This lizard is sometimes thought to be poisonous, but this is wrong, it is entirely harmless.

Range: From Texas to California in the Southwest.

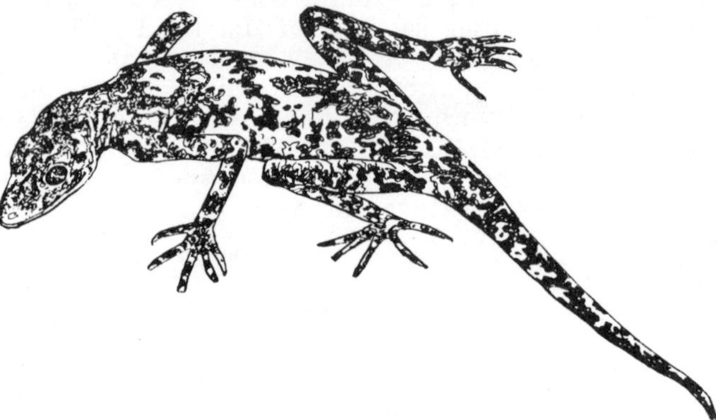

● AUSTRALIAN GECKO   *Gymnodactylus platurus*

Average size 10 inches; largest 14 inches; harmless.

Smooth skinned and mottled with dark brownish-yellow and white.

A night lover, although perfectly camouflaged for daytime travel on the ground or over logs. Have pads on their toes which adhere to any sticky surface. Like other lizards, can throw off their tail and grow another one. Finds no difficulty running upside down on the under surface of damp and clammy caves.

Make a sound like a cat's "meow."

Range: Australia.

Salamanders

● NORTHERN TWO-LINED SALAMANDER
Eurycea bislineata bislineata

Average size 3½ inches; largest 4½ inches; harmless.

Two dark lines, one on each side of the body, running from head to tail, identify this salamander. Body color varies—may be orange, brown or greenish.

Live under stones along the edge of streams and in the woods, especially if the weather is rainy. This is one of the salamanders without lungs; breathes through the skin.

Range: Northeastern United States.

● HELLBENDER
Cryptobranchus alleganiensis

Average size 20 inches; largest 27 inches; harmless.

Has a flat head and folds of skin along the sides; slimy skin.

The largest salamander in the United States. Many persons believe them to be poisonous, but they are entirely harmless, despite their formidable appearance. Are much the same as their giant cousin of Japan which grows to five feet in length. They live in streams where there are rocks to hide under.

Range: Eastern United States.

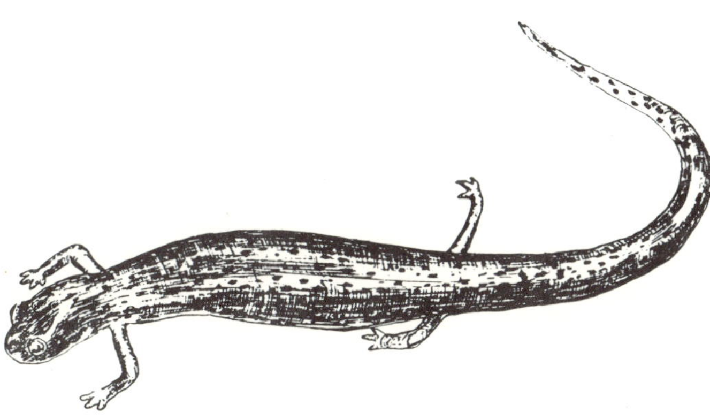

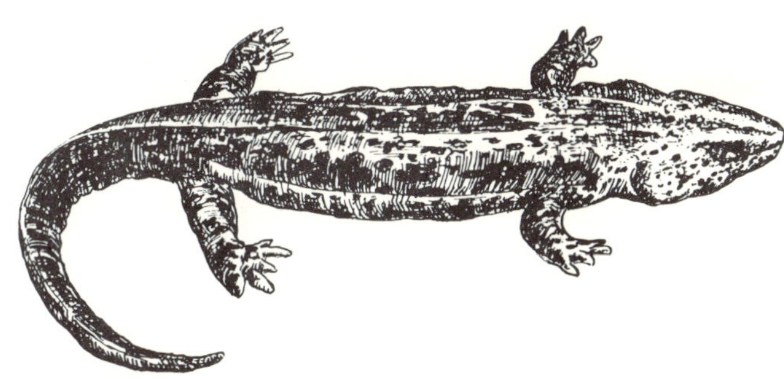

● FOUR-TOED SALAMANDER
Hemidactylium scutatum

Average size 2½ inches; largest 3 inches; harmless.

The distinguishing features are: four toes on each foot; belly marked with small black spots on ground color of white; constriction at base of tail, where the tail will detach itself if grasped by an enemy.

One of the smallest salamanders of the East. Usually found near the sea coast in the sphagnum bogs. While other salamanders have the ability to cast off their tails, as most all lizards, the Four-toed Salamander is the only one with provisions to cause the cleavage at a special place. Idea is that the tail, which continues to wriggle after being cast adrift, attracts the enemy, while the salamander escapes.

Range: Northeastern United States.

● GIANT SALAMANDER
Megalobatrachus japonicus

Averge size 3 feet; largest 5 feet; harmless.

Blackish with mottled back and lighter belly.

The giant of the salamander family. So large it would appear to be some other strange creature and difficult to compare to the tiny animals of America and Europe.

They live in rushing streams or under rocks in quiet pools. Come out at night and hunt their food. For the most part lie completely motionless in front of their abode, which they keep scrupulously clean.

Range: China, Japan and Tibet.

 # Salamanders 

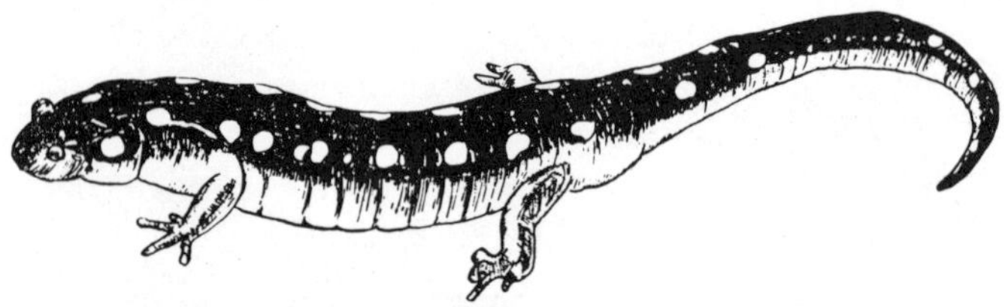

● SPOTTED
Ambystoma maculatum

Average length 6 inches; maximum 9 inches; harmless.

Resembles the Tiger Salamander, but differs in that there are two rows of light spots on the back. Much more abundant than the Tiger or Marbled Salamander.

A land salamander, only visiting pond water for egg-laying, in early Spring. Spends a good part of its life burrowing about under leaves and rocks. Prefers rotted logs or heavy underbrush.

Range: Northeastern United States.

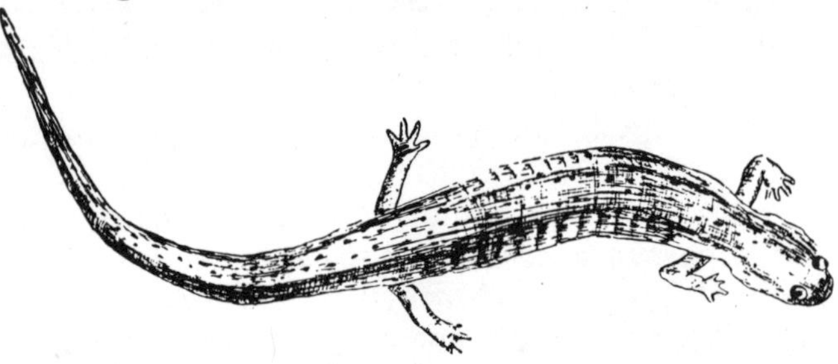

● DUSKY SALAMANDER
Desmognathus fuscus

Average size 4 inches; largest 5¼ inches; harmless.

Adults are gray or brown, streaked or spotted with irregular markings; when young, they have round light dots on the back; very old ones are uniformly dark.

The most abundant of salamanders, and smallest in the eastern states. They do not thrive well at high elevations, however. Seen commonly around spring houses and along the edge of streams.

Range: Eastern United States.

● MUD PUPPY
Necturus masculosus

Average size 8 inches; largest 12 inches.

Grayish-black with row of darker spots in loose pattern along the sides, flattened tail, large head.

Member of the Salamandar tribe inhabiting the rocky beds of streams. Feeds on insect larvae.

Range: Eastern United States.

● JEFFERSON'S
Ambystoma jeffersonianum

Average size 5 inches; largest 7¼ inches; harmless.

Dark gray or black, marked with sprinkling of small bluish silver dots; distinguished from Slimy Salamander by long slender toes.

Seldom seen by naturalists except in breeding pools in the Spring.

Range: Eastern United States.

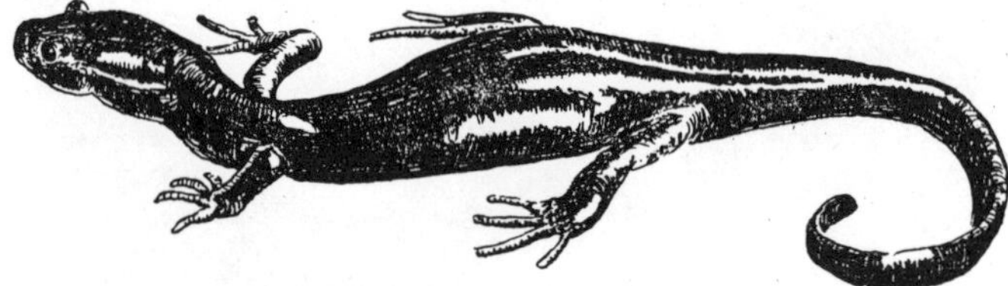

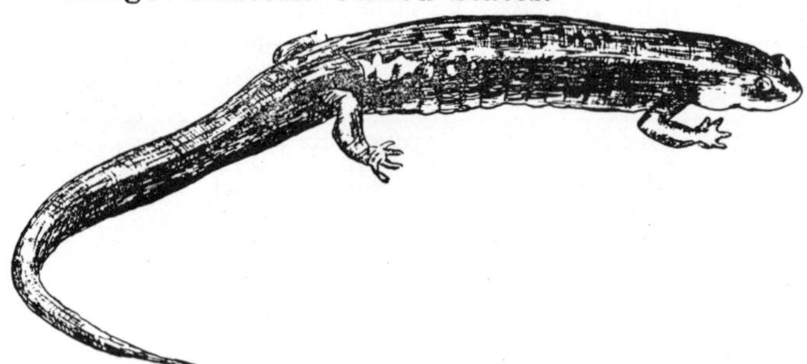

● ALLEGHENY
Desmognathus o₁ ochrophaeus

Average size 3 inches; largest 5 inches; harmless.

Resembles the Dusky Salamander a great deal. Best distinguishing mark is the straight-edged band of color down the middle of the back. This band may be yellow, orange, gray or brown.

A mountain salamander, preferring higher altitudes than the Dusky or others of the family. In size, is smaller than the others. Has the ability to scamper up and down steep inclines.

Range: Northeastern United States, particularly Alleghany Mountains.

● SLIMY SALAMANDER
Plethodon glutinosus

Average size 5 inches; largest 7 inches; harmless.

Glossy blue-black; sides heavily spotted with silvery-white. Few dots on back.

Generally found around logs or decaying piles of wood. A land creature, entirely. Name is derived from a secretion of stickiness coming from the skin when handled.

Feeds on snails and insects.

Range: In the east from New York to Florida and west to Texas.

 # Salamanders 

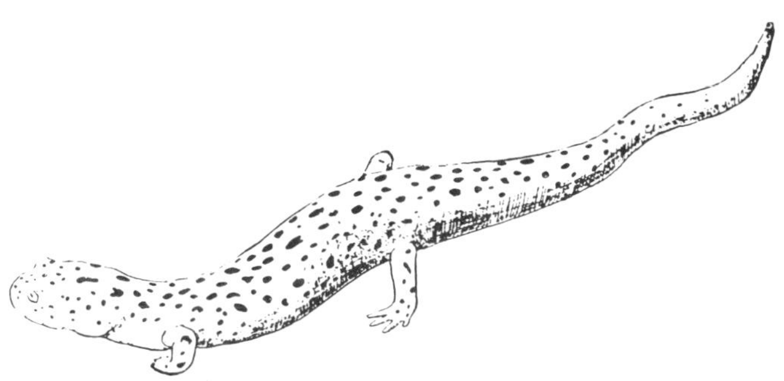

● RED SALAMANDER   *Pseudotriton ruber*

Average size 5 inches; largest 7⅛ inches; harmless.

Coral red to purplish-brown with dark irregular spots. Are found further from water than others of their kin, but must always be moist for they breathe through the skin.

This appealing little salamander makes a fine pet and will accept earthworms or finely minced hamburger as food.

Range: Eastern United States.

● LONG-TAILED SALAMANDER
Eurycea l. longicauda

Average size 5 inches; largest 6½ inches; harmless.

Strikingly marked in black and yellow with herringbone pattern.

A land-roving salamander, with a penchant for night movement. Usually can be found under stones and logs and in caves about springs.

A species on the rare side. Range mostly northeastern United States.

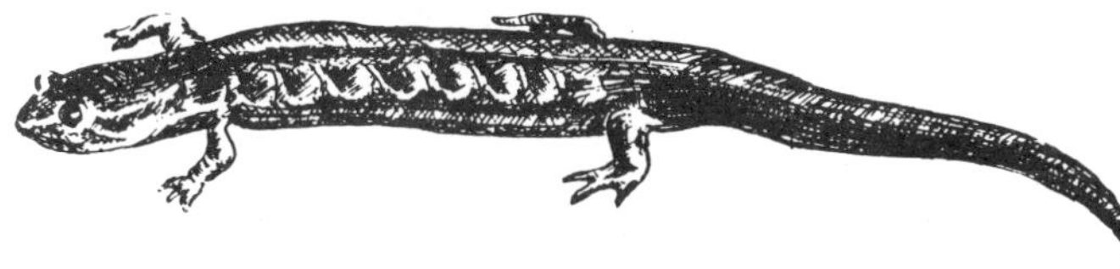

● SEAL SALAMANDER   *Desmognathus monticola*

Average size 4 inches; largest 5¾ inches; harmless.

Named for its sleek brown color, sometimes with darker markings. One of the larger members of the Dusky Salamanders. Solidly built; has a liking for mountain streams and waterfalls.

Range: Eastern United States.

● EASTERN RED-BACKED SALAMANDER
Plethodon cinereus cinereus

Average length 3 inches; largest 5 inches; harmless.

Two color phases: One bright red sprinkled with black; the other uniform black. Belly mottled like salt and pepper.

A land-loving salamander that seldom goes near the water. The young never do. Found throughout the woods in decaying logs. Common in Northern forests.

Range: Eastern United States.

● SPRING SALAMANDER   *Gyrinophilus porphyriticus*

Average size 5 inches; largest 7½ inches; harmless.

Purplish in color as a rule; although many are salmon color or brown.

Largest of the lungless salamanders, and the most stout-bodied. Live in cold mountain streams, preferably near waterfalls in heavily wooded country. They are very active when aroused and quite difficult to catch and handle.

Range: Northeastern United States.

● MARBLED SALAMANDER   *Ambystoma opacum*

Average length 3½ inches; largest 5 inches; harmless.

Body thick and short, lustrous black with brownish tinges on the underside of head and on legs and toes. Males bright white, females yellowish.

A salamander of the land which takes to water in fall rains. Found in locations not far from edge of ponds and lakes.

Range: Maine to Maryland in the Eastern United States.

Newts and Relatives

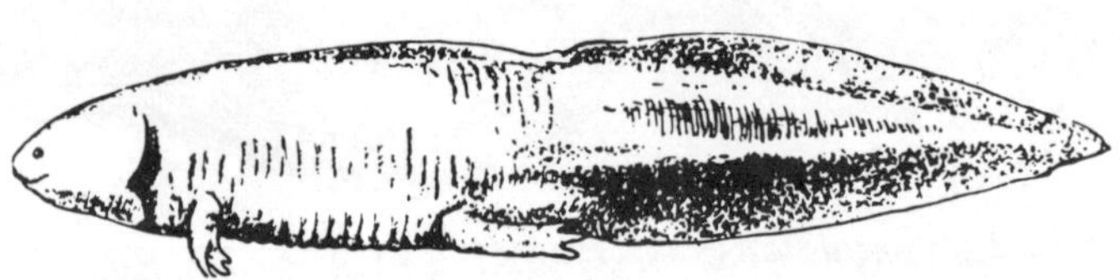

● **TIGER SALAMANDER**   *Ambystoma tigrinum*

Average length 4 inches; largest 12 inches; harmless.

Has blotchy yellow stripes or spots on dark body.

May develop either as a land or aquatic animal. Sometimes metamorphosis does not take place and they breed while in the larval or axolotl stage, shown above. (In some areas the axolotl is considered gourmet food). Others in the same species develop into fully formed salamanders.

Range: Widely distributed from Canada to Mexico.

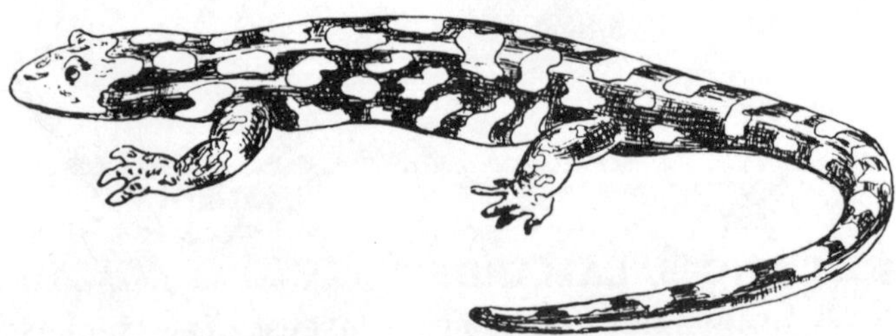

● **EASTERN TIGER**   *Ambystoma tigrinum tigrinum*

Average length 8 inches: largest 13 inches.

Marked with yellow spots. Belly and throat mottled with yellow.

Resembles the Spotted Salamander. A night crawling lizard, and thus rarely seen. Has an addiction to burrowing. Eggs are attached to leaves in ponds and stems of water plants.

Range: Pennsylvania, New York and New England.

● **PLEURODELE NEWT**   *Molge waltii*

Average size, 3 inches; largest 5 inches; harmless.

Olive above and yellow below with blackish markings. Distinguished by long pointed ribs, which sometimes are seen sticking through the body.

An aquatic creature, very hardy and known to live 20 years and more in captivity. Feed on insects and worms.

Range: Spain, Portugal and Morocco.

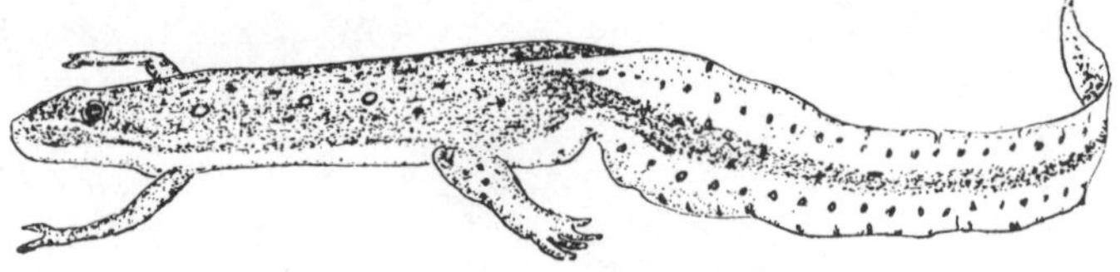

● **EASTERN RED-SPOTTED NEWT (Aquatic)**
Notophthalmus v. viridescens

Average size 4 inches; largest 5 inches; harmless.

Distinguished by number of red dots (one to eight) on each side of olive-green body. Belly is yellow with black dots.

Usually found attached to leaves of water plants, under water. Spends most of its life submerged.

Range: Eastern United States.

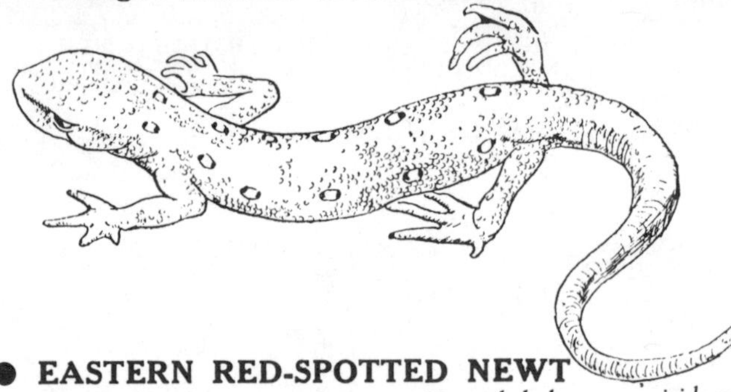

● **EASTERN RED-SPOTTED NEWT**
Notophthalmus v. viridescens

Land stage pictured above.

Average length 3 inches; maximum 4 inches; harmless.

Bright orange or scarlet spots on gray or brown background.

Lives on land for two or three years in the bright or colored form—and then becomes aquatic.

Most common in forests. Can be seen walking or running over leaves on forest floor.

Range: Found mostly in Pennsylvania.

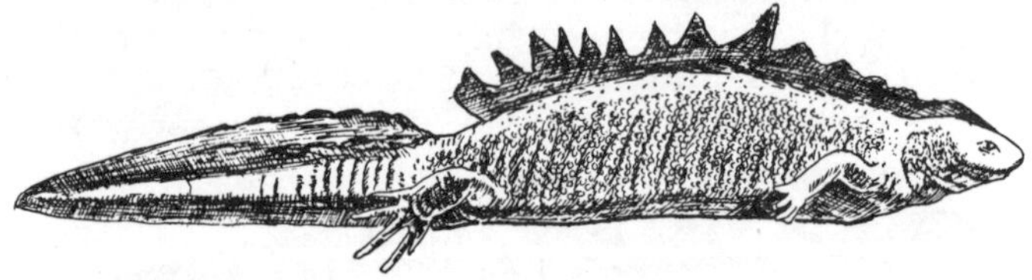

● **CRESTED NEWT**   *Molge cristata*

Average size 3 inches; largest 4 inches; harmless.

Brown, black or olive above with distinct black spots. A yellow vertebral line is present in female. Sides are speckled with white. Under surfaces bright yellow or orange.

The Newts as a rule, and the Crested Newt in particular, leaves the water after breeding season and retreats into a hole in the ground. Lives on insects and worms. Can be discovered by turning over stones near creeks.

Range: Native of British Isles, except Ireland.

Snakelike Lizards

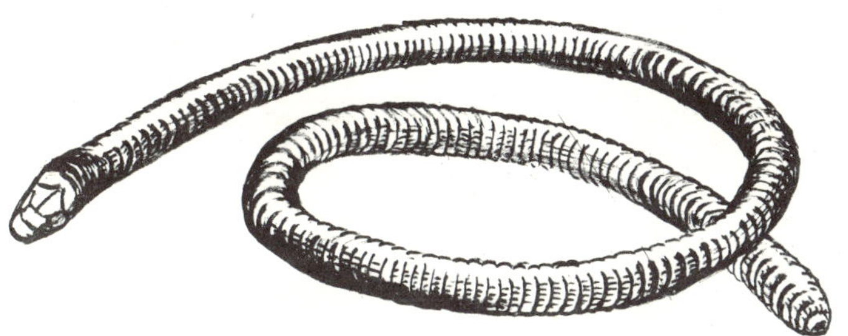

● FLORIDA WORM LIZARD — *Rhineura floridana*

Average size 7 inches; largest 12 inches; harmless.

The color is pinkish-gray to pale lavender.

This lizard is legless and the adult seems to lack eye or ear openings. These characteristics plus ring-like scales give it the appearance of an earthworm. It burrows in loose sandy soil, frequently found in plowed fields. Protect him! He's a good termite exterminator.

Range: Found only in Florida.

● IBERIAN WORM LIZARD — *Blanus cinerus*

Average size 10 inches; largest 14 inches; harmless. Black throughout with scales in horizontal rings.

A limbless lizard, which looks and acts like a snake. Feeds on insects. They burrow in the ground a good part of the time and rove more on cloudy days than sunny ones. On cool days they burrow as deeply as possible. Range: Spain, Portugal , Africa.

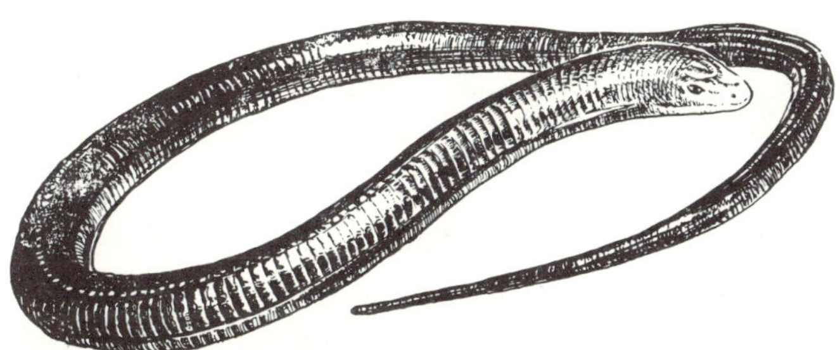

● EASTERN GLASS LIZARD

Also called GLASS SNAKE.

Average size 27 inches; largest 37½ inches; harmless.

Dark brown to black with a green dot in each glistening scale.

The Glass Snake is not a true snake, but a worm-like lizard, living for the most part under leaves and burrowing in the loose top soil. Feeding largely on insects, taken by grabbing, shaking until stunned.

A legend that they have the ability to fly to pieces and then reassemble, is not borne out by fact. Range: Found in southeastern United States.

● TWO-FOOTED WORM LIZARD — *Bipes biporus*

Average 9 inches; largest 10 inches; harmless. Dull purplish-brown. Lower half is yellowish-white. Body divided into numerous rings like an earthworm.

This creature is quite strange for a lizard. It is worm-like and almost blind. Two well-developed limbs with sharp claws are unusual and difficult to understand in the study of this combination worm, snake and lizard. Range: Only specimens found come from lower California.

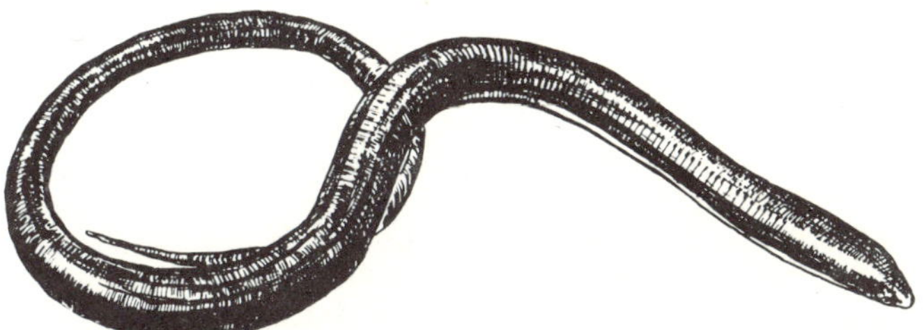

● EUROPEAN GLASS LIZARD — *Ophisaurus apodus*

Also called GLASS SNAKE.

Average size 3 feet; largest 4 feet, 1½ inches. Identified by the hard, bony feeling like glass or a varnished object when touched. Ebony black.

A true example of the limbless lizard family. The armor on outside, consisting of shell plates so well fitted they appear to be a solid skin. When the creature moves, it creaks. Has eyes, sharp and solid, with good vision. Also will throw off its tail with no blood letting like a lizard.

Range: Europe and Asia.

Cobras

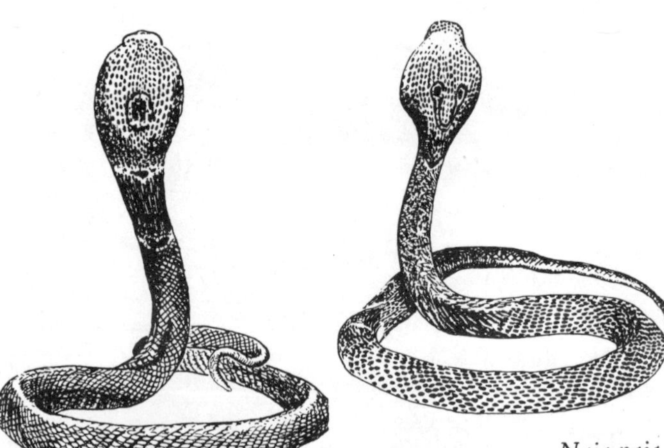

Naja naja

● **ASIATIC COBRA**

Also called COBRA DE CAPELLO, MONO-CELLATE COBRA.

Average size 5 feet; largest 7 feet; highly dangerous; poisonous.

Yellowish to dark brown with a spectacle marking on the hood. There is a black and white spot on each side of the lower surface of the hood. The Indian variety or Monocellate has one large black ring on the hood enclosing a paler area with black spot in the middle.

● **KING COBRA** *Ophiophagus hannah*

Average size 12 feet; largest 18 feet; deadly poisonous.

Olive or yellowish-brown, with ring-like crossbands of black. Have a ruddy hue about the chin and throat like a Florida tangerine. Eyes are bronze and brilliant.

This is the most dangerous of all snakes and of all living creatures on this earth. Not only has the King Cobra a large quantity of extremely powerful neurotoxin poison in his poison glands, which can kill the largest animal living, but is an aggressive snake, absolutely fearless and conducting himself as king of all animal life, which is true.

They are possessed of intelligence, far superior to other reptiles and are insolent in their behavior. They show anger, cunning and viciousness.

The King Cobra will rear usually about four feet. Does not spread a hood nor sway nor move, but stares fixedly at the object of its distaste.

Range: Distributed throughout Burma, Malay Peninsula, southern China and the Philippines as well as all of Malaysia.

● **ASP, EGYPTIAN COBRA** *Naja haje*

● **SOUTH AFRICAN COBRA** *H. hemachatus*

Egyptian Cobra (left). Color variable, generally brownish. In spite of large size, (up to 8 feet) and potent venom, are not overly aggressive.

South African Cobra, Ringhals (right), is sooty black, with light markings and ventral crossbars below hood. Can spit venom 6 to 8 feet, aiming at victim's eye. Intense pain, possible blindness, results. Smaller than the Egyptian, reaches 5 feet.

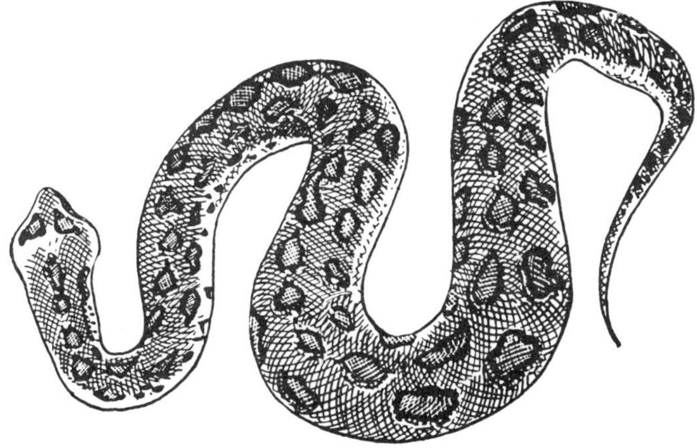

● RUSSELL'S VIPER
Vipera russellii

Also called TIC POLONGA.

Average length 4 feet; largest 5 feet; deadly poisonous.

Rich tan with three rows of black rings bordered with white, sometimes yellow, running entire length of body. Heavily bodied.

A sluggish Viper, rivaling the Cobra as being the deadliest of the Vipers. Can kill a chicken in 38 seconds; a dog in 26 minutes. A man can live for 14 days, however.

In striking, the snake eases along a foot or so, then springs from the ground. They produce a loud and intermittent hiss before striking.

A night-roving snake, preferring plains to mountains, living mostly on rats. In some parts of India very numerous.

Range: Found mostly in India, greatest number about Ceylon.

● TIGER SNAKE
Notechis scutatus

Average size 4 feet; largest 6 feet; poisonous. Olive or brown with dark crossbands.

One of the deadly serpents of the world, ranking with the Death Adder in viciousness and range of distribution. Found over a large area on dry and sandy soil, this snake will often show an antagonistic attitude.

Range: Australia.

● PUFF ADDER
Bitis arietans

Average size 3½ feet; largest 4½ feet; poisonous.

Brightly colored. Markings appear like black chevrons with yellow crescents.

This is the snake feared for its habit of lying in jungle foot paths. Unlike other snakes, they do not retreat on approach of humans, but strike when a target is within range. Many natives are bitten. The poison is not as deadly as other Vipers, although a lethal dose is sometimes received.

They make a loud hiss, such as the emitting of a puff of steam, when disturbed, thus receiving the name. Probably the most widely distributed of all Vipers.

Range: Mostly found in Morocco and Arabia.

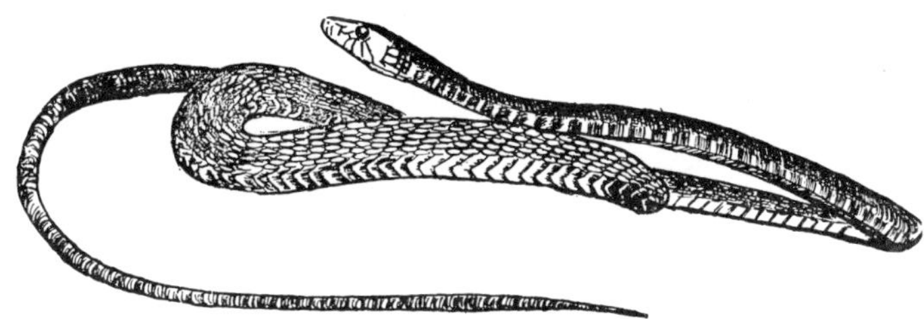

● GREEN MAMBA
Dendroaspis angusticeps

Average size 5 feet; largest 8 feet; extremely poisonous.

Color is uniform green, olive or black.

This snake is rated by many as the most deadly of all snakes. They inhabit hollow trees normally, but often are found coiled on tree branches. Feed principally upon birds, which they catch by striking with blinding speed. Can travel in the trees or on the ground at a fast pace.

When disturbed they often pursue the victim in a bold and aggressive manner. Many are the tales by natives, of hairbreadth escapes—and many who do not get away—when a Mamba is in pursuit. Of the various forms, the black-coated snake is most dangerous.

Range: Inhabits West, Central, and South Africa.

Dangerous Vipers

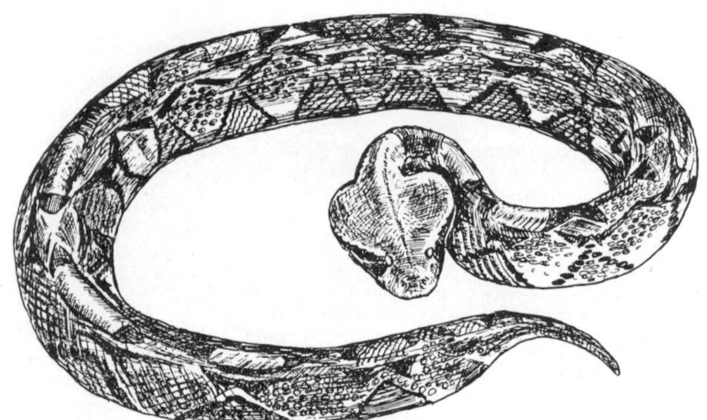

● GABOON VIPER
Bitis gabonica

Average size 4 to 5 feet; largest 6½ feet; poisonous.

A sinister snake. Thick body—eyes and nostrils on the top of snout, to lie buried. Geometric pattern of colorful patches in tans, blues and blacks with white edgings. Fangs may be 2 inches long. Hunts prey at night, sluggish in the daytime. Though ordinarily not aggressive, it has a highly toxic venom. If annoyed, flattens body, hisses and lunges at foe. Likes sandy, desert areas.

Range: Tropical Africa.

● RHINOCEROS VIPER
Bitis nasicornis

Also called RIVER JACK.

Average size 4 feet; largest 48 inches; poisonous.

Identified by two long horns on the snout. Very stout body. Considered most beautifully colored of all poisonous snakes. Upper surface looks like variegated velvet. Row of pale blue blotches on the back, each traversed by an orange band. The basic color is rich olive peppered with black. Horns are yellow.

A grassy and river-loving Viper, somewhat resembling the Gaboon Viper, yet preferring an entirely different terrain. Because of the great color combination, this snake has been said to resemble a giant caterpillar.

Range: Tropical West Africa.

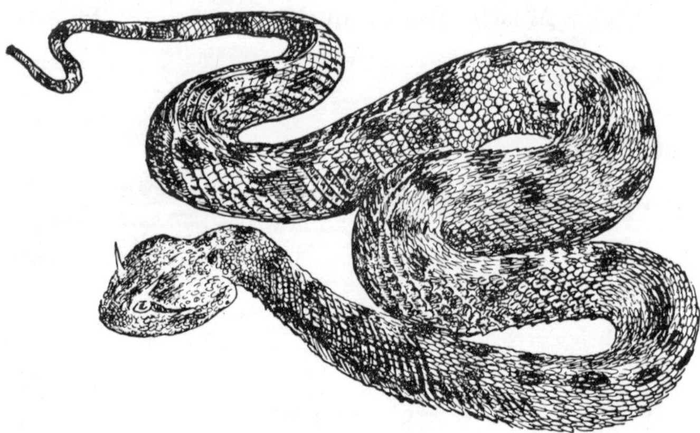

● ASP
Cerastes cerastes

Also called HORNED VIPER.

Average size 22 inches; largest 30 inches, poisonous.

Pale sandy hue; obscure markings. Over each eye is a sharp, upright spine.

A desert snake, born and bred to the hot sandy soil. Prefer to stay partly covered most of the time. This is the position they are in when stepped on by natives, thus receiving the name Asp. In some ways, their behavior resembles the Texas Sidewinder. The Asp, however, flattens its sides to dig sand and crawl, while the Texas Rattler moves by throwing loops. More active at night.

Range: Native of the Sahara Desert, Algeria to Egypt; also in Arabia and Palestine.

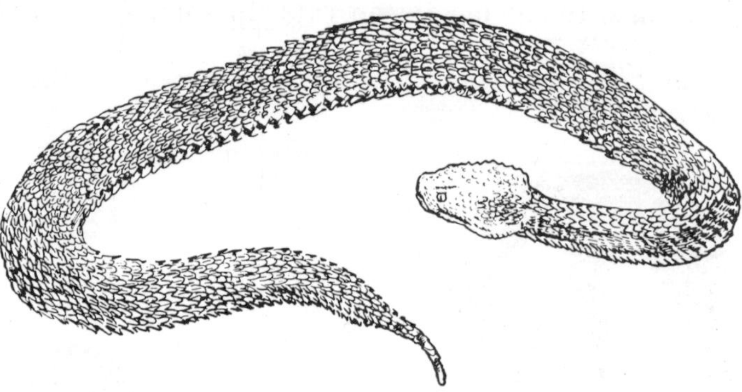

● SAND VIPER
Cerastes vipera

Average size 16 inches; largest 22 inches; poisonous.

Dull, sandy color, much the same as the Asp, except a bit smaller. Not quite so poisonous, but deadly just the same.

A thick-bodied snake of the desert, almost impossible to distinguish from the sand, unless it moves. Unlike the Horned Viper, a close cousin, there are no marking at all worth mentioning on the Sand Viper. When the body flattens out, the snake works sand over its back. Even the head disappears. This is like a mine planted in front of an enemy. When you step close to it, the fangs strike out and you're a goner.

Range: Mostly in Northern Africa.

Dangerous Vipers

● BUSHMASTER
Lachesis muta

Also called MUTE RATTLER, LASCABELA MUDA, SURUCUCU, MAPEPIRE Z'ANANNA.

Average size 8 feet; largest 12 feet; highly dangerous; poisonous.

Body pale brown, sometimes pinkish. Large dark brown blotches along body, wide on back, narrow on sides.

A bold and very dangerous snake, inclined to advance on victim, using great cunning to edge into an advantageous position for striking. Has no rattles, but vibrates tail in leaves or grass when alerted. Greatly feared as the world's largest viper.

Range: Central America, from Costa Rica to South America.

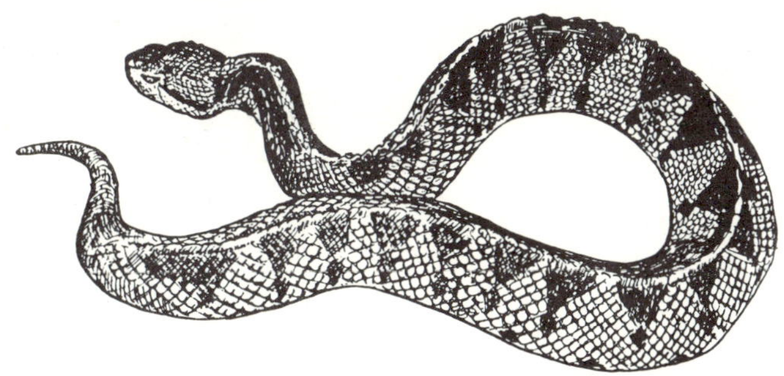

● JUMPING PIT VIPER
Bothrops nummifer

Also called MANO DE PIEDRA, TIMBA.

Average size 24 inches; largest 36 inches; poisonous, dangerous.

Gray or brown, with dark, black-edged blotches. Somewhat like a Bushmaster in markings.

Very stout body and large head, with exceedingly rough scales. Is a savage snake, leaping from two to three feet to strike; especially if cornered against a log or some object to jump from. The action is startling and the basis of considerable superstition.

Range: Distributed from Mexico south through Central America including Costa Rica and Northern Panama.

● COMMON VIPER
Viperus berus

Also called ADDER.

Average size 18 inches; largest 29 inches; poisonous.

Color pattern strong. There is a zigzag band down the back, usually sooty black. Another row of faded blotches on each side and a dark bar from the eye to the neck.

This is the most common of the poisonous snakes, especially in England. Generally timid, but can strike with lightning swiftness. Fortunately the poison is not as potent as other vipers, although it can be fatal if emergency treatment is not taken. They are usually found in dry grass or sheltered caves. Do not like dampness.

Range: British Isles and throughout Europe.

● HOG-NOSED PIT VIPER
Bothrops nasutus

Average size 24 inches; largest not known; poisonous.

Identified by upturned nose.

Range: A small species of Pit Viper found in the coastal region of South America, Tropical Mexico and Central America. Not as dangerous as some of the larger cousins, but the larger snakes can inject a lethal dose of poison.

 # American Pit Vipers 

● FER-DE-LANCE

Bothrops atrox

Average size 50 inches; largest on record 100 inches; highly poisonous.

Pattern of color differs widely in areas of concentration. Usually with light blotches along the back. Color varies from gray to brown.

The second largest Pit Viper, smaller only than the Bushmaster. Considered the most deadly snake of the West Indies and Tropical America.

A hardy snake, living and reproducing in captivity. They frequent both dry and swampy land and have no fear of populated centers.

Range: West Indies, Tropical America.

● JARARACA

Bothrops jajaraca

Also called MAXMILLIAN'S VIPER.

Average size 4 feet; largest 5 feet; very poisonous.

Identified by markings resembling an arrow pointing toward the nose and a row of symmetrical blotches along the back, ranging into dots toward the tail.

A thick-bodied and heavy snake, particularly quick and savage, of the Fer-de-Lance type, living for a good part of the time around the more squalid quarters in cities of tropical climate. Feeding on rodents, this snake has a good appetite. Will strike and kill humans when molested.

There are many sub-species of this reptile, probably 20 or more, with slightly different markings. All, however, are the same family and breed.

Range: Brazil and Northern South America.

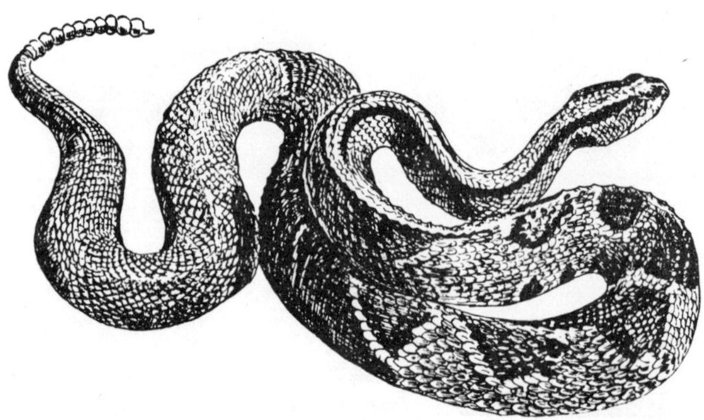

● CASCABEL

Crotalus durissus

Also called the TROPICAL RATTLESNAKE.

Average length 57 inches; largest 66¾ inches; very poisonous.

Pair of parallel stripes starting on head and running down back, distinguish this snake.

The Spanish version of the American Rattlesnake and considered most dangerous of all. Only slightly smaller than the largest, the Diamondback. Cascabel will often strike with little warning and **without coiling.** If aggravated will advance on an adversary, which a Diamondback never does.

Range: They inhabit the uplands of Mexico, down through Central and South America. Never found in swampy area.

● URUTU

Bothrops alternatus

Also called JARARACA de RABO.

Average size 4 feet; largest 5 feet; very poisonous.

One of the most numerous of the 40-odd species of lance-headed vipers found in tropical America. The other snakes on this page are of the same tribe.

A dangerous snake responsible for many snake bites every year. Beautifully patterned—dark markings like a French telephone, edged in white. Ground color brown.

Most unusual of the *Bothrops* family is the *Insularis* found only on an island, called Viper Island about 40 miles southwest of Bay of Santos. The reptiles feed entirely on the birds which nest there and have an extremely fast acting venom, developed undoubtedly to kill prey which is quick to escape.

 Rattlers and Tree Vipers

● SPOTTED RATTLESNAKE   *Crotalus triseriatus*

Average size, 20 inches; largest 24 inches; poisonous.

Grayish-brown, with several series of close set brown blotches on the back, faintly margined with white. On the tail, markings assume the form of rings. Head has a U-shaped blotch at the base. Belly is slaty-gray.

Frequents mountainous terrain and desires considerable elevation. One of the smaller of the Rattlers, yet none-the-less dangerous.

Found in the high plateaus of Mexico. Several have been found in Arizona.

● SOUTH AMERICAN RATTLESNAKE   *Crotalus terrificus*

Average size 5 feet; largest 7 feet; poisonous.

Ground color of rich yellow; brown rhombs, bordered with light yellow on the back.

Habits and markings greatly resemble the Diamondback Rattlesnake of North America. While they do not get as large, are quite dangerous. Unless cornered will not stand and strike or advance. Once coiled in defensive attitude, however, are tough customers to argue with. The most widely distributed of the Rattlers.

Found in Mexico, Central America and throughout South America.

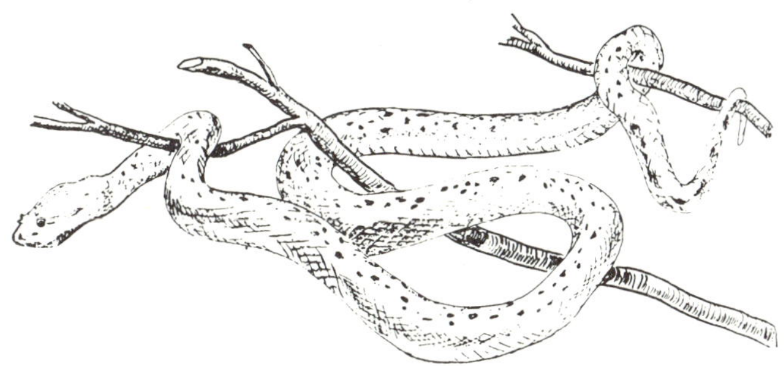

● SCHLEGEL'S PALM VIPER   *Bothrops schlegeli*

Also called EYELASH VIPER.
Average size 20 inches; largest 28 inches; poisonous.

Identified by two horn-like projections over the eyes.

A tree-dwelling Pit Viper. Ground color tan, green or yellow with scattered dark dots—varies in individuals. Although poisonous, are not aggressive and rarely has the bite been fatal.
Range: South and Central America.

● MARCH'S PALM VIPER   *Bothrops nigroviridis marchi*

Average length 30 inches; largest 40 inches; poisonous.

Green in color, small snake. Young are brown.

An arboreal Pit Viper of Honduras, inhabiting palm trees, for the most part. The bite of a large specimen can be fatal, although the poison is not as potent as other Pit Vipers.

Range: Central America.

Large Eastern Vipers

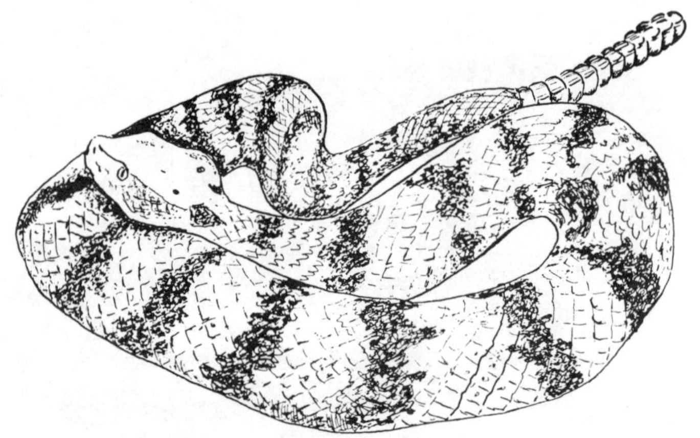

● **CANE-BRAKE RATTLESNAKE**
Crotalus horridus atricaudatus

Also called SEMINOLE RATTLER, SWAMP RATTLER, TIMBER RATTLESNAKE.

Average size 4½ to 5 feet; maximum length, 7 feet; poisonous.

Body is light gray, usually tinged with pink, and marked with black cross-bands. Tail usually black. Rusty stripe down the middle of the back.

Deaths from Cane-Brake Rattler bite are few; however, the bite of a large snake could be fatal.

Inhabits thickly wooded places, overgrown fields, and the edges of swamps. It once lived in the cane swamps, or cane-brakes in the southern United States; although the canes have nearly disappeared, the name "Cane-brake Rattlesnake" persists.

● **EASTERN DIAMONDBACK** *Crotalus adamanteus*

Also called DIAMONDBACK or HIGHLAND RATTLESNAKE.

Average size 4 to 5 feet; maximum length 7 feet 3 inches.

Greenish-gray, marked with blackish diamonds which are bordered with yellow. The diamonds become indistinct on the hind portion of the body.

The Eastern Diamondback Rattlesnake is found from North Carolina through Florida and westward to extreme eastern Louisiana. It is most frequently found in palmetto thickets, pine woods, abandoned fields, and live-oak stands, but may turn up almost anywhere.

● **TIMBER RATTLESNAKE** *Crotalus h. horridus*

Average length 45 inches; largest 74 inches; poisonous.

Bold black bands distinguish most conspicuous of the southern snakes. Northern specimens are much darker.

Highly dangerous, but not a vicious reptile. Should be approached with extreme care.

Food is small mammals and sometimes birds.

Found from the Atlantic Coast to Texas, except Florida and barely known in Maine.

● **TIGER RATTLESNAKE** *Crotalus tigris*

Average length 28 inches; largest 50 inches; poisonous.

Markings of ring-like pattern and tawny bone hue, give the name "Tiger" to this Rattler.

A very mean and dangerous snake. Inhabiting a narrow portion of the United States and Mexico from Phoenix, Ariz., to Sonora, Mexico. While not as large as other members of the Diamondback clan, it is fully as dangerous because of a mean disposition.

Range: Southwestern United States and Mexico.

Large Western Rattlesnakes

● **WESTERN DIAMONDBACK**   *Crotalus atrox*

Average length 4 feet; maximum length 7 feet, 5 inches; poisonous.

Distinguished by diamond pattern on back and great size.

The most deadly snake in North America, with the possible exception of the Eastern Diamondback. There is little to choose between them. The Western species is possibly two inches greater maximum length, although average size is less. Strikes a deadly blow and injects poison of the blood-destroying type. The bite of a large snake is usually fatal unless expert attention is at hand.

Range embraces all of the West from Missouri to California, as far north as Nevada and south to southern California. Extreme eastern Texas has none. The West is heavily populated generally.

● **RED DIAMOND RATTLESNAKE**   *Crotalus ruber*

Average length 45 inches; largest 6 feet; poisonous.

Distinctly reddish, usually a brick-like hue. Obscure markings.

Apparently a mild-mannered snake for all it's poisonous nature. Slow to show anger and seldom rattles. Found in open brush country. Is calm and quiet in captivity.

The Red Diamond is a powerful snake, often found wandering in the open with no sheltering bush or rock crevices to retreat into.

If approached this snake will assume a threatening attitude, although remaining quiet—and sounding its rattles only occasionally, sometimes not at all. If not attacked, will show no further antagonism toward strange humans.

When left alone, the Red Diamond Rattler crawls along in leisurely manner, through sage and over the sand and rock terrain.

Range: Mostly in lower California.

● **MOJAVE RATTLESNAKE**   *Crotalus scutulatus*

Average length 37 inches; largest 62 inches; poisonous.

Recognized by enlarged scales on top of the head and round dorsal patches. (Spots on back).

A desert-loving Rattler, found mostly on the edge and sometimes deep in the desert country of southern Nevada, western and southern Arizona and highlands of Mexico. Also found in Texas and New Mexico.

Like all Rattlers, are dangerous. Fortunately, however, since they seldom stray into populous areas, few people encounter them.

Range: Western and Central United States.

● **PACIFIC RATTLER**   *Crotalus viridis oreganus*

Average size 40 inches; largest 62 inches; poisonous.

Sometimes brown and sometimes greenish or grayish with large blotches along the back, edged with a paler hue.

A dangerous snake of the far west, ranging throughout California and north through Oregon and Washington. Also on the islands off the California coast.

Noted for their habit of congregating in large numbers in the fall to den up for the winter in rock caves.

Range: Pacific coastal areas.

Very Dangerous Rattlesnakes

● **ROCK RATTLESNAKE**   *Crotalus lepidus*

Average length 22 inches; largest 48 inches; poisonous.

Greenish or greenish-gray hue marked by widely separated and narrow rings of black.

Identified by regularly spaced black splotches with serrated edges on the back.

A dangerous snake, although smaller than the average Western Rattler.

A rare snake, which has been found along the region of the Mexican boundary and to the west through New Mexico and Arizona.

Headquarters for the tribe is Texas, although the range includes New Mexico and southeastern Arizona and some parts of the Mexican highlands.

● **BLACK-TAILED RATTLESNAKE**

Crotalus molossus

Average length 40 inches; largest 56 inches; poisonous.

Distinguished by black tail, from 6 to 10 inches up.

This is a handsome snake with dark, oblong blotches edged in yellow. The general body hue is a rich yellow. The tail is sooty black.

Widely found in the southwestern states of America.

Native of Southern Mexico and Southwestern Texas and the highlands of Mexico. Much the same in habits as the Diamondback. Is a cousin—and close one—of the Diamondback, although not as large. Very dangerous.

Range: Southwestern United States.

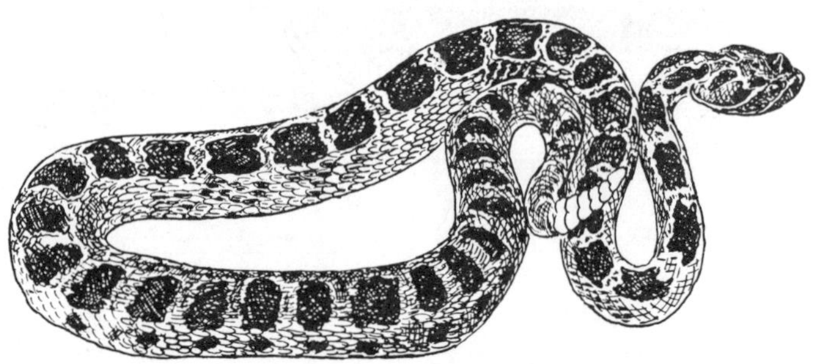

● **GREAT BASIN RATTLESNAKE**

Crotalus viridis lutosus

Average length 38 inches; largest 60 inches; poisonous.

Fairly thick in body and marked with irregular blotches on back.

A highly dangerous snake ranging in the Great Basin area of the United States. The Plateau region from the Rockies to the Sierras is the natural habitat. They are also in eastern Oregon and southern Idaho. Sub-species of the Western Rattlesnake.

Range: Western Mountain area.

● **PRAIRIE RATTLESNAKE**   *Crotalus viridis viridis*

Average length 36 inches; largest 5 feet; highly poisonous.

Can be recognized by the unusual markings on the head and blunt nose.

The Great Plains Rattlesnake, common throughout the Plains area of the United States and into Canada.

Dens up in Winter in rock pits. Travels widely in Summer. Dangerous snake.

Range: Mid-West United States.

Small Rattlesnakes

● MITCHELL'S RATTLESNAKE *Crotalus mitchelli*

Also called SPECKLED RATTLESNAKE.

Average length 33 inches; largest 46 inches; highly poisonous.

Markings and coloring similar to the Red Diamond Rattlesnake. Blotches over back. Well developed rattles.

This is the Rattlesnake variation found mostly on the Lower California uplands. Sometimes seen as far north as Nevada and in central and western Arizona.

Is a dangerous snake, considered one of the most vicious of the Pit Viper family.

Range: Southwestern United States.

● MASSASAUGA *Sistrurus catenatus*

Also called BLACK SNAPPER; SWAMP RATTLER.

Average length about 2 feet; largest on record, slightly over 3 feet; poisonous.

Red-brown or black blotches (21 to 37) along mid-line of back. Two rows of similar but smaller markings along side. Ground color, gray to brown. Belly dark, heavily blotched with black.

Rather mild tempered but dangerous if aroused. Venom is highly toxic and has caused death in some instances.

Staple food is mice. Also eats frogs.

Most common in bogs and swamps, although in summer they do move to higher ground.

Found in central New York and western Pennsylvania, Ontario, Michigan, Ohio, Indiana, Illinois, Iowa, Missouri and southeastern Nebraska.

● PYGMY RATTLESNAKE *Sistrurus miliarius*

Also called GROUND RATTLER or OAK-LEAF RATTLER.

Average size 18 inches; maximum length 35 inches at Miami Serpentarium; poisonous.

Body is usually gray, with several rows of blackish or brown spots. Belly is cream or white, with black spots.

The bite produces much pain and swelling, but is seldom if ever fatal. There are no recorded deaths from the bite. A bad tempered fellow.

From North Carolina southward throughout Florida, and thence westward to Texas, Arkansas, and Missouri.

The Pygmy Rattlesnake is characterized by a very tiny rattle, which can be heard but a few feet away.

● SIDEWINDER *Crotalus cerastes*

Average length about 18 inches; largest 32 inches; poisonous.

Cream color. Has conspicuous hornlike projection over each eye. This protects eye from blowing sand when snake is buried or half buried.

Not as deadly as larger Rattlesnakes, but a very dangerous snake. Possible to stumble on one by accident.

Inhabits the desert areas of the West. Is curiously adapted to locomotion in loose sand. To move forward, the snake's head, with neck sharply bent, is brought forward through the air and set down. The body is then brought forward in a rolling motion and laid down in front of the head. Thus the body is never dragged. The trail looks like a series of "J's" in the sand—lying parallel. They move only at night.

Range: Western desert country.

Moccasins and Copperheads

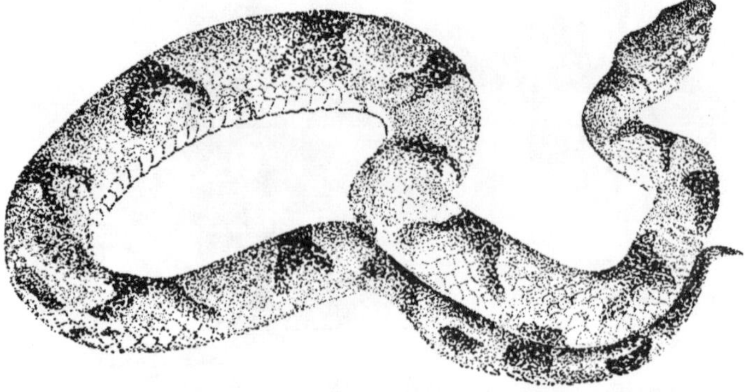

● **COTTONMOUTH** *Agkistrodon piscivorus*

Also called WATER MOCCASIN.

Average length 20 inches; largest 44 inches; poisonous.

Moccasins have many color variations and are difficult to detect and describe. General characteristics are thick heads, keeled scales with dorsal blotches, sometimes in diamond shape and sometimes in bands. Colors vary from coppery to black. The young are most colorful. A Pit Viper. The pit is discernible between eye and nostril. Eyes are elongated. All non-poisonous Water Snakes have round eyes. Paired fangs are located in upper jaw beneath the pit.

A very dangerous snake. Unpredictable and undependable. They can strike from the ground or under water. They have been known to charge humans, striking repeatedly while following the intended victim's retreat. Other times the snake is completely docile. They can coil and strike from the surface of the water. They often vibrate their tail against the ground when aroused and, opening wide the mouth, display a white interior with fangs in place. A terrifying object. The poison is fatal if received in sufficient quantity.

Feed on small mammals, frogs and fish.

Common on banks of fresh water streams flowing into salt water. Salt water marshes also inhabited by this snake.

Range: Lowlands of southeastern United States.

● **MEXICAN MOCCASIN** *Agkistrodon bilineatus*

Also called CANTIL.

Average size 26 inches; largest 38 inches; poisonous, very dangerous.

Head is dark with a narrow but vivid yellow stripe beginning at the snout, passing over the eye and ending at the back of the head. Also there is a broader stripe extending along the upper line. General color is dark brown or dark gray.

It has the same general character as the Water Moccasin of the southeastern United States.

● **COPPERHEAD** *Agkistrodon contortrix*

Also called COPPERHEAD MOCCASIN, HIGHLAND MOCCASIN.

Average length 2 feet; largest on record, 4 feet 2 inches; poisonous.

Pinkish, tan, or yellowish-brown in color, with darker cross-bands of reddish-brown or chestnut. Head coppery or reddish-brown.

Seldom if ever fatal to adults in good health.

Most common in wooded uplands, such as the Appalachians, often abundant even in well-settled areas.

Range: Massachusetts and southern New York southward to northern Florida, thence westward across Texas and northward to southern Iowa, Illinois, and Indiana. Within this area four races are recognized, differing slightly in details of pattern.

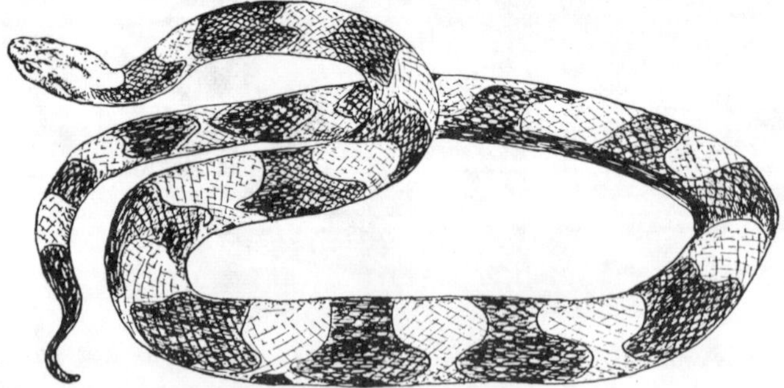

● **NORTHERN COPPERHEAD**
Akistrodon contortrix mokeson

Also called UPLAND MOCCASIN; CHUNKHEAD; PILOT SNAKE.

Average size, 30 inches; largest, 4 feet 5 inches; poisonous.

Reddish-brown or chestnut; darker than Southern Copperhead. The pattern of crossbands is sometimes indistinct. Belly is darker than back and mottled with gray.

As a whole the Copperhead is inoffensive, always retreating and seldom striking. However, their bite is dangerous and should be treated as a Rattlesnake bite. When aroused they rattle their tails like a Rattlesnake.

Range: Throughout the highlands of eastern United States.

Coral Snakes

● **EASTERN CORAL SNAKE**   *Micrurus f. fulvius*

Also called THUNDER SNAKE.

Average length 28 inches; largest 43 inches; captured by Samuel Stockton, St. Petersburg, Fla.; poisonous.

Black snout as far as the eyes, then a yellow band, next black. From there, alternating wide bands of red and black, separated by narrow rings of yellow. Looks polished. The bands are continuous, encircling the body.

This snake is as poisonous as a cobra, but is less dangerous only because it is less aggressive and because the fangs are shorter—in fact so short that shoes or clothes afford fair protection. They do not coil to strike and usually lie flat on the ground, hiding behind leaves or burrowing. Watch out for them in early morning. Don't underestimate this snake. Bites infrequent, but high percentage of bites are fatal.

There are several harmless snakes which mimic the vivid coloration of the Coral. Among North American varieties, yellow rings bordered on each side by black, denotes "harmless". Generally too, the belly is white or blotched.

Range: North Carolina to Southern Florida and west to Texas.

◉ **ARIZONA CORAL SNAKE** *Micruroides euryxanthus*

Also called SONORA CORAL SNAKE.

Average size 12 inches; largest 18 inches; poisonous.

Black snout and color combination much the same as Eastern Coral Snake. First three rings are the color key in the above two snakes. Eastern: black, yellow, black. Arizona: Black, yellow, red.

• This is the pigmy of Coral Snakes. Inhabiting areas of Arizona and New Mexico. Because of smaller size is less dangerous, yet the poison is even more toxic than the southeastern variety. Only difference, there is not so much of it.

Usually keeps well hidden except just after sunrise. Dangerous to handle.

Range: Southwestern United States.

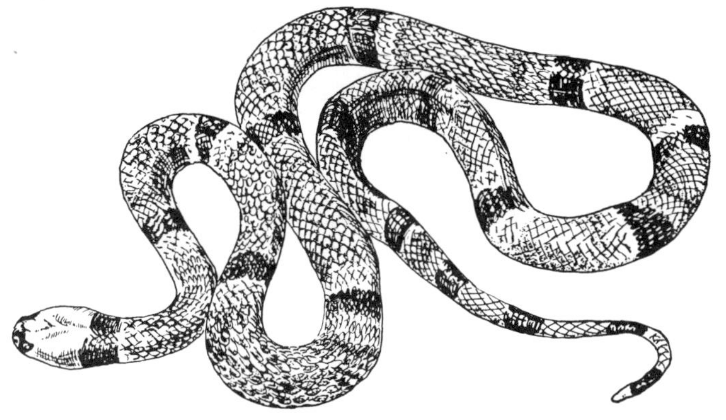

● **CENTRAL AMERICAN CORAL SNAKE**

Micrurus nigrocinctus

Average size 24 inches; largest 4 feet; poisonous.

Brilliantly colored. Noted by wider than usual red rings. Color pattern similar to the Coral Snakes in general.

A burrowing snake, seldom dangerous unless stepped on. Will use short fangs and hold on if held in the hand and forced to bite.

Habitat from Guatemala to Panama.

● **WIED'S CORAL SNAKE**   *Micrurus corallus*

Average size 2 feet; largest 3 feet; very poisononous.

The pattern is alternate broad bands of brick red and purplish-black—within the black bands are two narrow rings of yellow. It has a red snout with a black band behind the eyes.

A burrowing type. Not aggressive, but the bite is deadly.

Range: Tropical South America.

Imitation Coral Snakes

- ### SCARLET KING SNAKE
Lampropeltis doliata doliata

Also called FALSE CORAL.

Average size 15 inches; largest 24 inches harmless.

This is the most beautiful of the King Snakes. The rings continue around the belly as in the Coral Snake. However, the "harmless" rule applies; the yellow bands are touched only by black ones—wide red bands alternate with this combination. The narrow, pointed head is red.

The Scarlet King is found throughout the southeastern United States. Other members of the same tribe, rather similar in appearance, are found in the mid-Atlantic States and in California. One authority claims that at least one species of King Snake can be found in every state except Washington. The California Mountain King Snake—same color scheme, grows larger, sometimes over 3 feet.

Diet consists of mice, insects, lizards and other snakes, including Rattlers (they are immune to the venom).

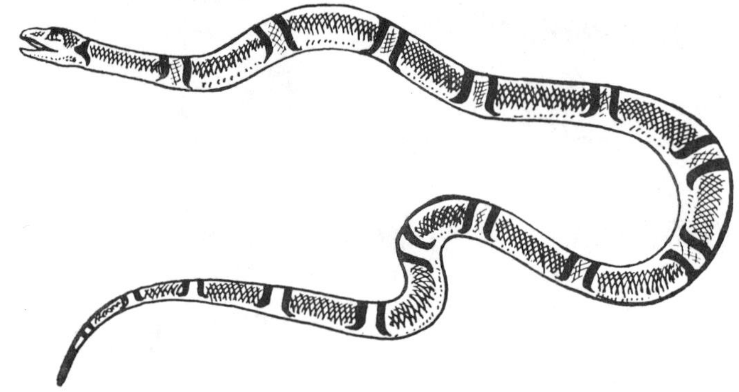

- ### SCARLET SNAKE
Cemophora coccinea

Average size 15 inches; largest 25 inches; harmless.

Broad scarlet rings, separated by yellow rings that are bordered on each side by black. Has a white belly.

This snake is often mistaken for the poisonous Coral Snake, although it is fairly easy to tell them apart. The rings are spaced much farther apart on the Scarlet Snake and the head is red with a black band just back of the eyes. A Coral Snake has a black head.

A constrictor snake, feeding on small mice and living mostly in the bark of trees or in logs. Often found around habitations.

- ### SOUTH AMERICAN CORAL MIMIC
Oxyrhopus trigeminus

Average length 20 inches; largest possibly 30 inches; harmless.

Mostly black with broken rings of red and yellow.

Sometimes taken for a Coral Snake, but can easily be recognized as innocuous because the areas of color do not completely encircle the body. They are not as sharply defined as in the Coral Snake.

Widely distributed in South America.

Range: Southern Mexico and Central America.

- ### TROPICAL AMERICAN CORAL MIMIC
Eryrolamprus aesculapii

Average length 20 inches; largest 26 inches; harmless.

Wide black and narrow yellow bands, completely encircle body.

Often mistaken for a Coral Snake because the bands are highly colored and make complete circles of the body.

Widely distributed throughout tropical America.

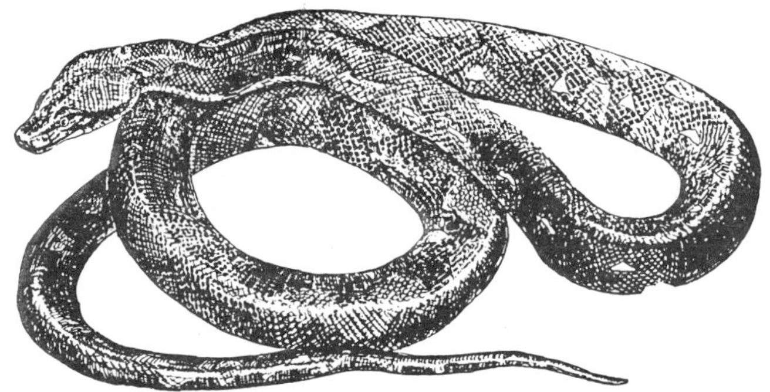

● REGAL PYTHON
Python reticulatus

Average size 22 feet; largest known 32 feet; dangerous to man; edible as food.

Have a glistening skin, intricate yellow-brown and black markings. Head is brown with narrow black line extending backward from the snout. Eyes are red with vertical purple.

The Regal Python is the world's largest snake. An average specimen will weigh 225 to 250 pounds. They kill and eat all manner of mammals including goats, leopards and sheep. They kill by constriction, throwing three coils around the victim after first grasping with their jaws. This pressure stops breathing, but does not break the bones.

When a Python has eaten, a cool and shady nook is selected and the snake does not stir again for a week or more. During this time it is sluggish and an easy prey for hunters.

Range: Malaysia.

● INDIAN PYTHON
Python molurus

Average size 14 feet; largest on record 25 feet; dangerous.

Basic color yellowish-brown with saddles of darker brown on the back. Single white stroke down center of the head.

One of the most beautiful of the Pythons, with vividly marked body, rather heavy set for the great length of the species. This is the third largest snake of the world. Likes to be near water and can stay submerged for a half hour.

Found in southern India, China, the Malay Peninsula and Java.

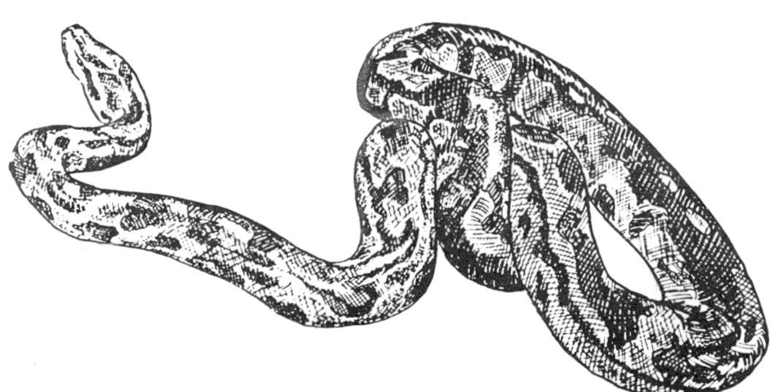

● AFRICAN ROCK PYTHON
Python sebae

Average size 12 feet; largest 16 feet; dangerous.

Pointed head as compared to other Pythons; more distinctly formed markings, rather oval in shape. Basic colors brown and yellow. A dark horizontal splotch on both jowls.

Fourth largest of the Pythons and one of the rarest. Seldom seen in captivity. Spends a good deal of time in rocky terrain, taking to trees when in search of birds.

Range: Central and South Africa.

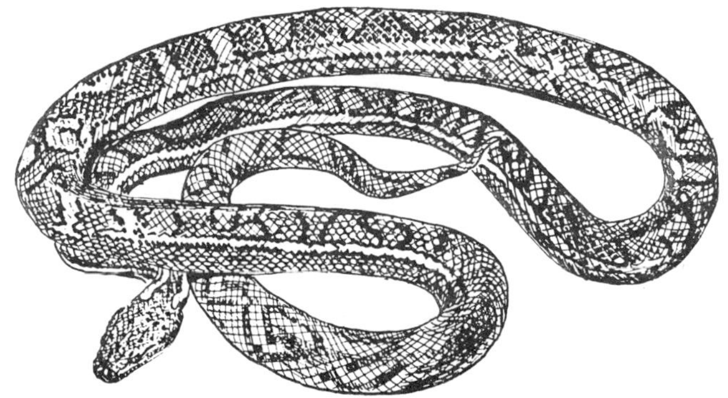

● DIAMOND PYTHON
Morelia argus

Also called CARPET PYTHON.
Average size 8 feet; largest 12 feet.
Light yellow to dark brown with a basic pattern of brownish saddles along the back. Distinguished by four dots on the upper lip.

A tree-loving Python, quite active in daylight, but when not hungry, or just finished eating, may be found rolled into a ball and balancing on the branch of a tree.
Range: Australia.

● BLOOD PYTHON
Python curtus

Grows to about 9 feet. Is much smaller than the Indian Python. It, too, is fond of water and is found near rivers and streams. Feeds on rats and mice.

Considered edible in some parts of the world. Easily caught for it is a sluggish reptile.

Range: Malaya & Malay Archipelago.

● ROSY BOA
Lichanura roseofusca roseofusca

Average size 24 inches; largest on record 3 feet, 2 inches; non-poisonous.

Bluish-gray basic color with a pattern of contrasting zig-zag longitudinal stripes from nose to tip of tail, usually dull brown in color.

A slow-moving deliberate snake of California, quite harmless and never aggressive. When disturbed they do not attempt to bite, but roll themselves into a ball with head buried in center. Can be picked up that way. Make excellent pets. Feed on mice, which they kill by constriction.

Range: California and Arizona; southern half of Mexico.

● ROYAL PYTHON
Python regius

Also called BALL PYTHON.

Average size 3 feet; largest 5 feet; harmless.

Body color chocolate-brown with patterns like rosettes of varying size, vividly margined with yellow.

The pet snake of the Pythons. Very beautiful and gentle. Have a habit of rolling into ball when frightened. Can be handled and fed without fear of damage. Almost impossible to induce this snake to bite a human.

When the Royal Python forms a ball, its head and neck are tucked into spaces between the folds, making a compact sphere about the size of a bowling ball. They may be rolled on the floor a distance of 12 feet or more with a light push of the hand.

Make exceedingly interesting and instructive pets.

Found in West Africa.

● EMERALD TREE BOA
Boa canina

Average 3 feet; largest about 6 feet; harmless.

Emerald-green above and lemon-yellow below. A series of enamel-white markings along the back and down the side, furnish a broken camouflage.

Considered the quietest and gentlest of the boas, especially Tree Boa Constrictors. Can be handled without a show of temper. Feed on small mammals, well adapted to captivity.

Range: Brazil and the Guianas.

Giant Boa Constrictors

● SOUTH AMERICAN BOA CONSTRICTOR

Constrictor constrictor

Average size 7 feet; largest 16 feet; dangerous to man.

Light yellow with dark brown saddles on the back, extending from head to tail. Intricate patterns on sides; belly, pale yellow.

The Common Boa Constrictor is a tree snake, as are most all Boas. They climb by encircling the trunk with the hind part of their body and then stretch the fore part up and encircle a branch. In crossing from tree to tree, sometimes up to 10 feet is extended between boughs.

They capture prey by hiding in the tree above and dropping on the unsuspecting victim, crushing with constrictions.

Range: Mexico to South America.

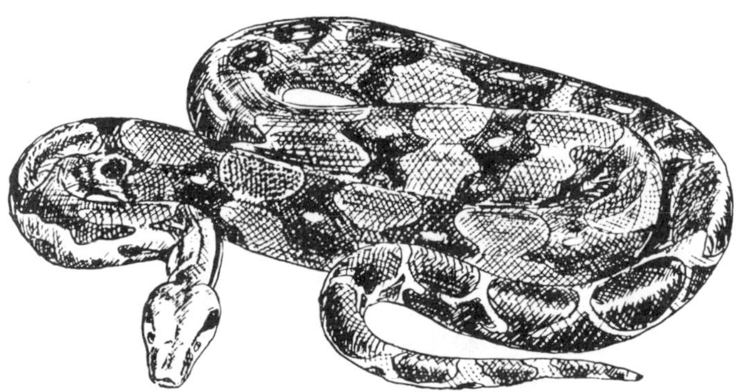

● CENTRAL AMERICAN BOA *Constrictor imperator*

Average size 5 feet; largest 12 feet.

Dusky brown with saddles of darker hue, each marked by one white spot. Heavy-bodied snake.

Another and smaller of the Water Boas or Anacondas of the tropics. This specimen is considered even more gentle than the larger brother, Yellow Anaconda. Feeds on small birds and mammals caught along the river banks.

Range: Southern Mexico and northern South America.

● ANACONDA

Eunectes murinus

Also called WATER BOA.

Average size 12 feet; largest on record 20 feet; dangerous.

Dark green with round black spots.

Largest of the Water Boas, and a giant among snakes, the Anaconda is the subject of many fabulous stories in South America. They are reported to be 25 and even 30 feet in length, although no authentic record of a specimen over 20 feet has ever been proven.

An aquatic snake and constrictor, they feed on small mammals found ordinarily along the banks of rivers.

Not adverse to taking anything they can swallow.

Range: Central America and tropical South America.

● YELLOW ANACONDA

Eunectes notaeus

Average size 10 feet; largest 14 feet.

Basic color is yellowish-green with irregular and ragged blotches on the back, like saddles.

Much the same as the full-size Anaconda, in habits and actions. A water-dwelling reptile, only occasionally found on land. Kills prey by constriction, but is not antagonistic.

Range: South America.

Small Boa Constrictors

● CUBAN BOA
Epicrates angulifer

Also called MAJA.

Average size 7 feet; largest 11 feet; dangerous.

Pale brown on the back with scattered dark blotches on the sides and irregular brown blotches on the back. Has large glittering eyes. On the whole a sinister-looking snake.

The largest of the snakes of the West Indies and of the family *Epicrates*. A very ill-tempered snake and one that never loses its diabolical disposition. Has a vicious-sounding hiss.

Hunted extensively in Cuba for the hide. Is the largest snake in either Cuba or Puerto Rico, the only places where it is found. Becoming scarcer now, as the trail is fairly easy for natives to follow in the fields.

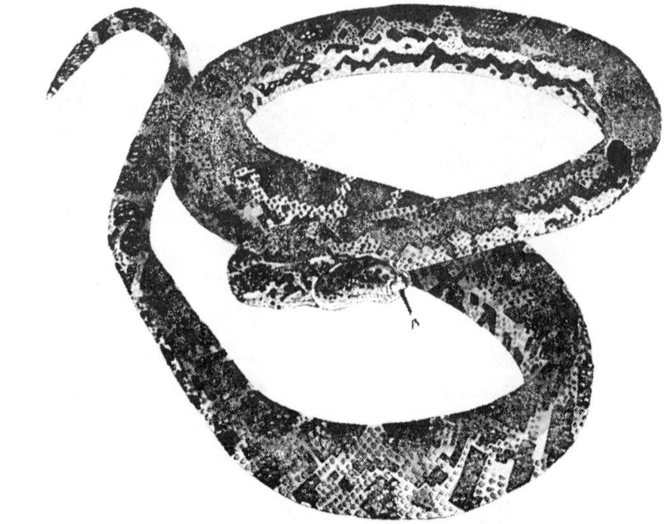

● BAHAMA BOA
Epicrates striatus

Average 5 feet; largest 8 feet; non-poisonous.

Identified by narrow zig-zag black and gray transverse bands producing a marbled effect.

Very little is known of this rare island snake. Usually they are quite harmless and gentle and do not give evidence of antagonism when encountered. Feed on rodents and frogs. Spend most of their time in water or damp places, although equally at home in the woods.

Found only in the southern Bahama Islands and San Domingo.

● MADAGASCAR TREE BOA
Sanzinia madagascariensis

Average size 5 feet; largest 7 feet; dangerous.

Distinguished by large head and slender neck, has long and vicious-looking teeth. Appears much like a poisonous snake. Color pattern varies, usually a dusky-green or purple with yellowish or brown saddles over the back.

Probably the most vicious of the Boa family. Not at all like the ground and water Boas of larger size. Has a very bad temper and teeth to back it up. Although there are no poison glands behind the fangs, this snake, dropping out of a tree and getting hold of one with the teeth, can quickly throw several constricting coils and harm a person.

Found only on the island of Madagascar.

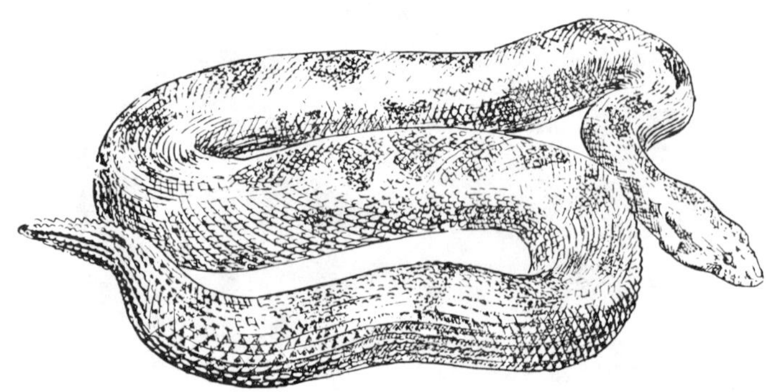

● ROUGH SCALED SAND BOA
Gongylophis conicus

Average 3 feet; largest 4 feet; non-poisonous.

Pale brown with wide undulating band narrowly bordered with ruddy yellow. Somewhat resemble the Tic Palonga or Russell's Viper.

A hardy snake with very rough scales; difficult to handle. Spend their time burrowing in the sand and only come out for feeding. They take mice, rats, sparrows and such food. Are not antagonistic and do not bite.

Found in India.

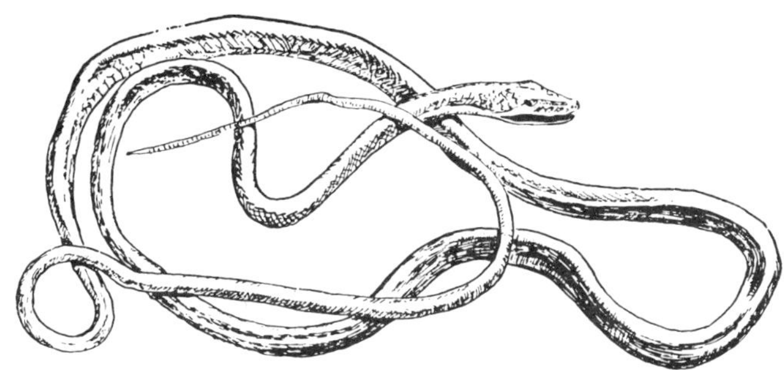

● LONG-NOSED TREE SNAKE   *Dryophis nasutus*

Average length, 4 feet; largest 6 feet; slightly poisonous.

Distinguishing characteristics: Greenish in color, exceptionally large head for small diameter of body.

A lizard-hunting tree snake, which lives in the trees all year. Has an uncanny ability to swallow lizards or small mammals, much larger in circumference than itself. This is a rear-fanged snake, with poison ducts just sufficient to numb its prey.

Range: Ceylon, Malaya, East Indies.

● DIAMOND BACK   *Coluber diadema*

Average length 4 feet; largest 5 feet; harmless.

Scales glossy pattern in contrasting brown and cream color. Gives the appearance of painted enamel.

Rare snake of Africa, with habits much the same as the American Blacksnake. Not much is known of them.

Range: North Africa.

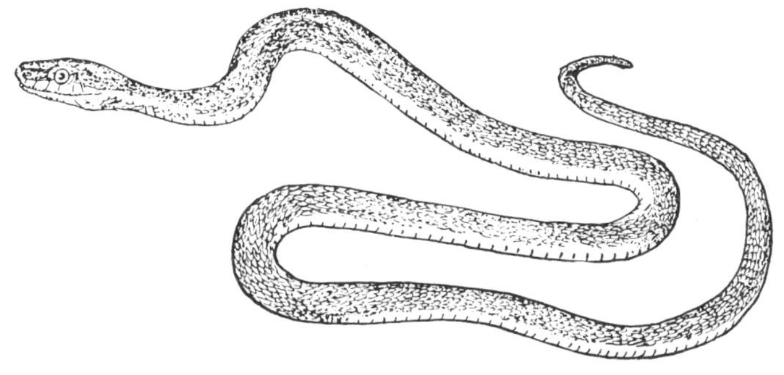

● KEELED GREEN SNAKE   *Opheodrys aestivus*

Also called ROUGH GREEN SNAKE.

Average length 28 inches; largest known 42 inches; harmless.

Slender, long-tailed snake; uniform light green above, whitish, yellow-tinged belly. Scales are prominently keeled.

Harmless and mild-tempered, but sometimes they bite if molested. Non-poisonous.

Usually seen in shrubs and low trees. Inclined to move mostly at night.

Eats insects exclusively.

An unusual habit of this snake is to protrude the tongue rigidly from the mouth, without spreading the fork tip, or rapidly waving that organ as most snakes do. This is usually while the snake is in motion. The tongue is a pale flesh color, readily noticeable.

Found from Connecticut to Florida and the Gulf states northward to Kansas.

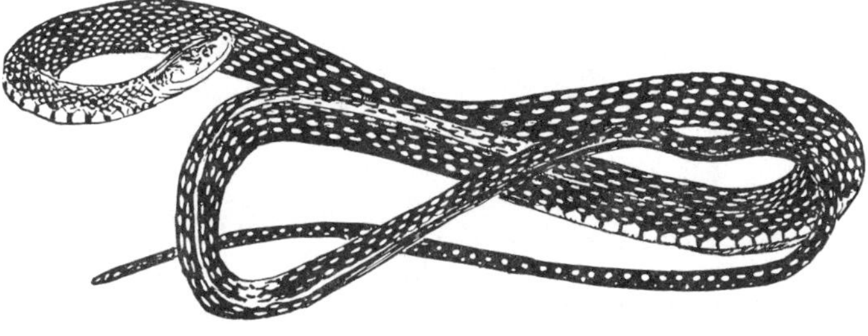

● GREEN SPOTTED RACER   *Drymobius margaritiferus*

Average size 4 feet; largest 5½ feet; harmless.

Identified by large head, with yellow lips and curving mouth. Body entirely covered with cream-colored spots on a green background.

A tree-loving reptile which can match exactly the pattern made when the sun shines through the branches. Living all its life on the tree branches, this snake hunts out bird's nests and chases small birds. Will grab a lizard when opportunity presents.

This is a very pretty snake, with markings so perfect they have been compared to an oriental pattern, carefully set down and then lacquered. Nearly every scale of the back and sides carries a single bright spot approximately in the center.

As Ditmar has said, the effect is of a large and lustrous serpent, symmetrically dotted with a bright blue, striking design. The spots are closer spaced and in linelike rows near the tail.

Range: Texas southward through Venezuela.

● SOUTH AMERICAN RIVER SNAKE
Cyclagras gigas

Average size 4½ feet; largest 6 feet; harmless.
Brownish-yellow with variegated pattern near tail. Yellow belly and whitish at throat.

A water snake of the large rivers in South America. Considered rare in comparison to other snakes of the tropical waterways. Feeds on fish and small mammals.

Range: Tropical South America.

● FOUR-LINED SNAKE
Elaphe quatuorlineata

Also called FOUR-RAYED SNAKE.

Average size 4 feet; largest 6 feet; harmless.
Yellowish ground color with a black band on each side of the back and a similar band beneath, somewhat resembling the Chicken Snake.

One of the largest of European snakes, somewhat plentiful in the old weeded areas about the castles on the Rhine and such rivers. They are considered beneficial and not molested except by uninformed people.

Range: Southern Europe.

● SLENDER TANTILLA
Tantilla gracilis

Also called MITER SNAKE.

Average size 8 inches; largest known 9 inches; harmless.

Brownish color with flat dark head, salmon-red belly.

Smallest of the Black-headed or "Crowned Snakes." Like the others, is secretive, hiding under stones and logs. They do not bite when handled but usually try to squirm into a crevice and hide in captivity.

Range: Found in Missouri, Kansas and south to Texas.

● AUSTRALIAN BLACK SNAKE
Pseudechis porphyriacus

Also called PURPLE DEATH ADDER.

Average size 4½ feet; largest 6 feet; poisonous.
Blue-black with a row of scales on each side of abdomen which are red.

Spreads poorly developed hood, Cobra fashion, but venom less toxic. A very abundant species, found in every type of terrain. Feeds on rats and birds.

Range: Australia.

● EMORY'S RAT SNAKE
Elaphe guttata emoryi

Also called GREAT PLAINS RAT SNAKE.

Average size 3 feet; largest 4 feet; harmless.
Ashy-gray with series of brown blotches on back, narrowly margined with black. Belly yellowish-white with dull gray blotches.

The smallest of the Rat Snakes and quite slender. A gentle type, rarely nervous and takes well to captivity, eats small rats and mice. Likes to climb low trees.

Found west of the Mississippi river to New Mexico.

● COMMON BULL SNAKE *Pituophis melanoleucus sayi*

Average size 5 feet; largest on record 9 feet, according to Ditmars; non-poisonous.

Basic color is yellowish with large squarish blotches appearing on back.

One of the best known of all American snakes, mostly because of size and wide distribution. Is an exceedingly heavy snake for length. Likes the prairie country most of all and is quite numerous in the Great Plains region.

Despite its size, the Bull Snake is docile, although when cornered they put up a threatening attitude. In captivity they are unusually tame. The spectacular size and color pattern make them quite interesting pets.

They are regarded as a friend to the farmer in the Middle West and often are sought in wild country to be released on farm land. They have a large appetite for rodents and especially pocket gophers.

Range: Throughout the central United States from Mexico to Alberta, Canada.

● FOX SNAKE *Elaphe vulpina*

Also called PINE SNAKE.

Average size 40 inches; largest 5½ feet; non-poisonous.

Ground color, yellowish to light brown with series of blotches on back. Belly yellowish-white.

Somewhat resembles the color pattern of a Timber Rattlesnake and sometimes mistaken for a venomous reptile. A heavy snake for length. When cornered it vibrates tail in dry leaves which resembles a rattlesnake warning.

Range: Northern states along the Great Lakes to Indiana.

● PACIFIC BULL SNAKE

Pituophis m. catenifer

Average size 4 feet; largest 4 feet 7 inches.

Dull yellowish-brown with small, square reddish-brown blotches on back. On the sides is an obscure series of smaller blotches. Belly is yellowish with small dark blotches on the edges.

Prefer the sterile and warm areas of the land. As a whole are not antagonistic as are some other Bull Snakes. When greatly disturbed will hiss and rattle the tail.

Range: Pacific Coast region, west of the Sierra Nevada Mountains.

● CORN SNAKE *Elaphe guttata*

Also called RED RAT SNAKE, RED CHICKEN SNAKE, RED HOUSE SNAKE.

Average size 3 feet; largest on record 6 feet, 1 inch; non-poisonous.

A pattern of up to 40 red-brown blotches, edged with black on a basic color of light reddish-brown, sometimes gray.

This is one of the most beautiful of American snakes. Lives mostly in fields of corn, thickets or around farm buildings. Usually moving at night, is also seen in shady situations in daylight. When cornered will hold ground, vibrating the tail and hissing loudly.

Is a constricting snake, feeding mostly on rodents.

Range: New Jersey to Florida and west to New Mexico, in the south.

 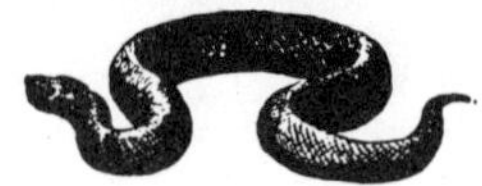

Black Snakes

● **EASTERN YELLOW-BELLIED RACER**

Coluber constrictor flaviventris

Average size 4 feet; largest 5 feet, 10 inches; harmless.

Bluish or greenish snake. Belly very light blue, sometimes yellow.

A large snake of the Blacksnake-Racer family. Has a habit of racing over the tops of bushes which sometimes gives rise to the theory that it "chases" people. This is not borne out in fact. Eats frogs and toads and small mammals.

Characteristic of Racer is to crawl with raised head.

Range: From Rocky Mountains east through Ohio.

● **NORTHERN BLACK RACER**

Coluber constrictor constrictor

Average size 3 feet; largest 5 feet, 11 inches; non-poisonous; will bite, ripping skin with sharp jaw.

Satiny black; chin and throat milky white. Smooth scales.

One of the largest snakes of the eastern United States. Although the name implies it is a constrictor snake, it is not. Food is frogs, eggs and other snakes.

Supposed to have the power of hypnosis, this is not held to be true by scientists. Usually inhabits dry and open country and shuns humans; taking off at great speed when disturbed.

Range: Eastern United States.

● **PILOT BLACKSNAKE**　　*Elaphe obsoleta obsoleta*

Also called BLACK CHICKEN SNAKE, MOUNTAIN BLACKSNAKE.

Average size 5 feet; largest 9 feet; harmless.

Ebony black throughout body. Faintly keeled scales.

One of the four largest snakes in North America. Known for a habit of invading chicken houses in search of rodents and making off with eggs when they are found.

Sometimes mistaken for common Blacksnake, but is larger and has a wider head. When startled has a loud hiss and makes a pretense of striking.

Found throughout the eastern United States from New York to Florida and west to Texas.

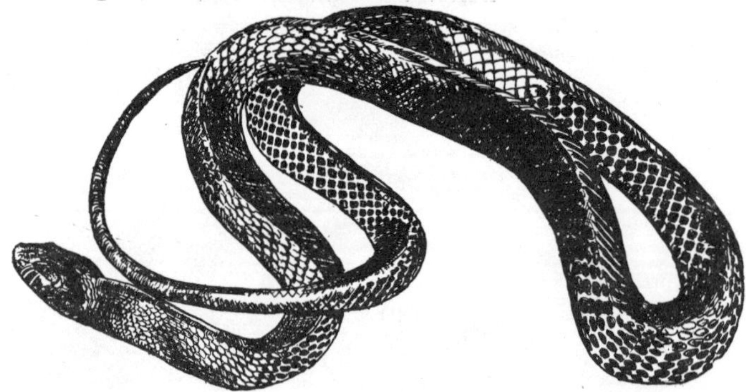

● **INDIGO SNAKE**　　*Drymarchon corais couperi*

Also called GOPHER SNAKE.

Average size 5 feet; largest 7 feet, 9 inches; non-poisonous.

General color bluish-black, darker toward the tail. Looks polished.

One of the largest of the non-posionous North American snakes. It favors high and dry land, often making its home in a burrow dug by gophers. Adapts well to captivity and because it has a gentle nature, is a favorite with circus snake charmers, and as a pet.

There is an Eastern and a Texas Indigo snake, very similar in behavior and appearance. The western variety has a brownish cast. A close relative lives in South America.

Range: South Carolina to Florida and west to Texas.

Rat Snakes

● **YELLOW RAT SNAKE** *Elaphe o. quadrivittata*
Also called FOUR-LINED CHICKEN SNAKE.

Average size 4 feet; largest 7 feet; harmless.
Yellow in color with four lines of dark brown running the entire length of the body. Belly yellow.

Found in barns and chicken houses. Travels in daylight looking for rats and mice. Compared to other snakes they are bold and fearless. When cornered they coil and strike as if to bite, vibrating their tail. In captivity they are quite tame.

The Rat Snake or Chicken Snake is a great climber, often found high in oak trees. They are fond of rafters in barns and poultry houses where they watch for unsuspecting mice or rats.
They also like eggs and young chickens, often swallowing three or four at a time. They swallow their prey whole and in the cases of eggs, break the shells by contraction, digesting shells and all.

They are bold and fearless. When surprised, assume a striking pose, moving the tail so rapidly it sounds like a rattler. They strike, but have no fangs.

When cornered the Rat Snake emits an odor offensive to most persons. This comes from a gland at the base of the tail.

Range: Southeastern United States.

● **INDIAN RAT SNAKE** *Ptyas Korros*
Average size 5 feet; largest 9 feet; harmless.
Identified by the sharp ridge on the back, running the entire length of the body. General color is brown.

Named because of an enormus appetite for rats. They are protected in many parts of India. A fine is levied on persons killing them. A highly nervous type, giving an imitaton of a Cobra when disturbed. They are absolutely harmless, however.
Range: Malay Peninsula and Java.

● **GLOSSY SNAKE**

Arizona elegans

Also called FADED SNAKE.
Average size 30 inches; largest 3 feet, 9 inches; non-poisonous. Docile.

Pale colored and spotted with small flat-topped head; series of dark-edged blotches down the back on a basic color of cream or pale brown. Belly is yellowish-white; sides are of a marbled appearance.

Resembles a Bull Snake, but smaller. Likes the desert country and hides out in daylight. Color is faded to blend with the sand and background of habitat. Feeds on lizards.
Range: Found in Kansas, Oklahoma and Texas.

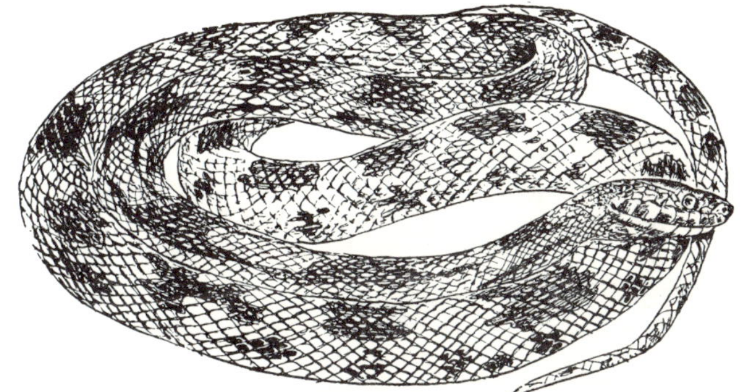

● **GRAY RAT SNAKE** *Elaphe obsoleta spiloides*
Also called SPOTTED CHICKEN SNAKE.
Average size 4 feet; largest 8 feet; harmless.
Ground color of gray with a pattern of large blotches, black and dark brown. Belly yellowish, blotched with gray.

A close relative to the Pilot Blacksnake. Inhabits chicken houses and farm yards. Very fond of chicken eggs, which are raided at every opportunity.

In natural abode the Gray Rat Snake prefers ledges on the hillsides. Often they can be seen stretched out on the tops of bushes sunning themselves. When surprised they appear to throw themselves toward a crevice where they disappear with agility.

They catch and kill their prey by constriction, the larger snakes often feeding on rabbits, of a size to nearly grown. They are often found in the same vicinity as Rattlesnakes, although the two species appear to live together without undue antagonism.

Range: Starts at North Carolina and throughout the Gulf Coast states.

Milk Snakes and Relatives

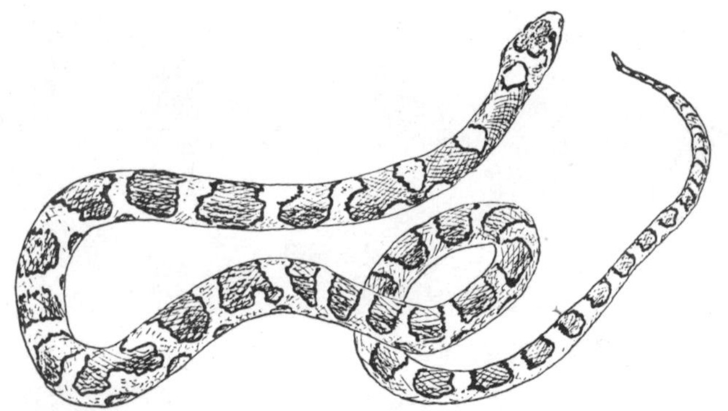

EASTERN MILK SNAKE
Lampropeltis doliata triangulum

Also called SOUTHERN MILK SNAKE.

Average size, 30 inches; largest on record, 3 feet, 6½ inches; harmless.

Basic color gray with a series of blotches down the back. A row of smaller blotches on the sides and a row of spots on the belly, which is white with an assortment of small black squares. Usually a Y-shaped patch on back of head.

Belonging to the King Snake family, it is a night prowler. Found in all kinds of terrain from damp to dry. There is a myth that these snakes take milk from cows, which is not based on fact. When cornered will assume defensive pose and bite, chewing the finger or toe that is grasped. Usually choose mice for their diet, but are also fond of small snakes.

Range: Eastern United States and Southeastern Canada; Maine to Florida.

LOUISIANA MILK SNAKE
Lampropeltis d. amaura

Average size 14 inches; largest 25 inches; non-poisonous.

The smallest and brightest of the Milk Snakes. Color scheme mimics the dangerous Coral Snake, but as with other imposters, "Red doesn't touch yellow", so he's a good fellow. Red pointed snout, black head.

Range: Southern Gulf States.

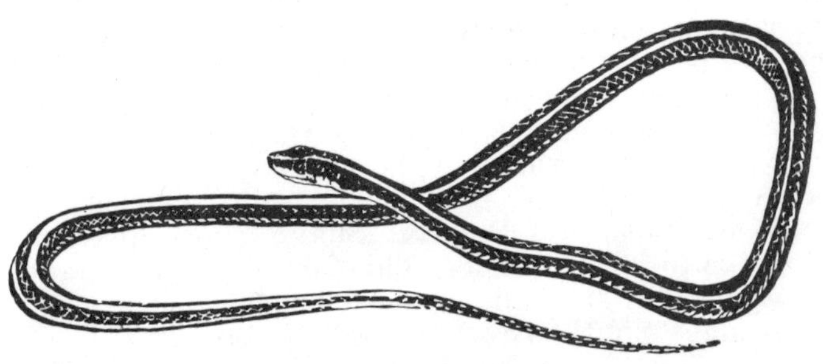

EASTERN RIBBON SNAKE   *Thamnophis sauritus*

Average size 16 inches; largest 33 inches; harmless.

Basic color is gray or greenish-black. Three stripes run the length of snake, one on back and one on each side. These are vivid yellow. Narrow yellow mark in front of each eye.

Probably the slimmest of American snakes. Usually no thicker than a lead pencil. Likes damp places and found along the border of mountain streams or ponds. A good swimmer and spends a lot of time in the water. If necessary can dive beneath the surface.

Will attempt to bite if handled, although it can do no damage.

There are four members of the Eastern Ribbon clan. All similar with slight color variations.

Range: Eastern United States from Canada to Florida and west to Mississippi.

PINE SNAKE   *Pituophis melanoleucus*

Average size 4 feet; largest 8 feet, according to Ditmar.

Dull white on back, very white on belly. A series of black blotches down the back. Head resembles a turtle, somewhat. In Florida the markings are more brownish.

Catch birds and raid birds' nests for food. Also eat rodents.

Range: Eastern states from New Jersey to Florida.

Coachwhip Snakes

● EASTERN COACHWHIP

Masticophis f. flagellum

Average size 5 feet; largest on record 8 feet, 7 inches; will strike, but not poisonous.

Head and forepart of body dark brown or black, color lighter toward the tail. The coloration of body gives the appearance of a braided whip.

The Eastern Coachwhip is the largest of the Whipsnake family and the only member found in the Eastern part of the United States. The longest ever measured was 8 ft. 7 in.; killed by David G. McCoy in 1926 after it struck at him without provocation from the limbs of a tangerine tree. The incident occurred in a grove that is now the site of the Continental Can Co. plant in Auburndale, Fla.

They can move through brush or on open ground with great rapidity. They are nervous and savage and vibrate their tails and strike like a Rattler when annoyed. They prey mostly on lizards and mice. Although they will bite, are not poisonous.

Range: N. Carolina to Fla. and west to Texas.

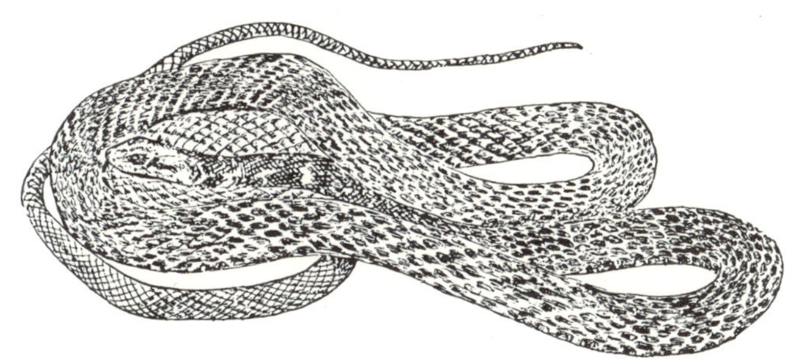

● RED RACER

Masticophis f. piceus

Also called WESTERN BLACK RACER.

Average size 38 inches; largest 6 feet; non-poisonous, but will bite and tear flesh.

Found in two distinct colors—in the one, backs are completely black. A red variety has black cross-bands on anterior portion. Belly pale. Always has a white stripe horizontally between the eye and the nostril.

One of the Whipsnake family inhabiting the West. Bold and active, traveling in daylight and hibernating at night. A nervous and rather savage snake, although not poisonous. They kill Rattle-snakes.

Can travel equally fast on the ground or over the tops of bushes.

Range: Lower and Central California, east to Utah and south into Mexico.

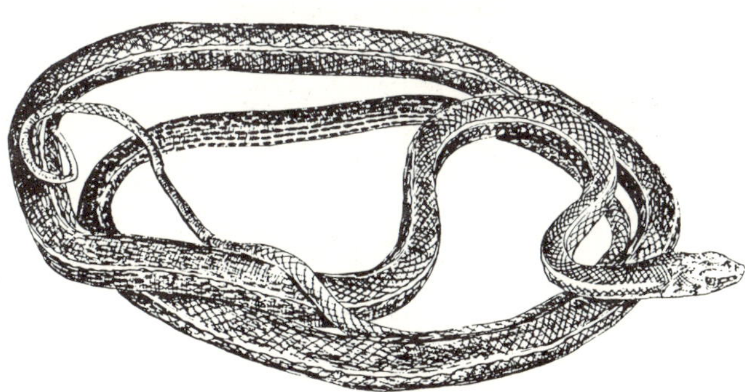

● CALIFORNIA STRIPED RACER

Masticophis l. lateralis

Also called CALIFORNIA STRIPED WHIP-SNAKE.

Average 3 feet; largest 4 feet; non-poisonous.

Dark brown or black, with a single yellow stripe on each side of body. The stripes have a narrow margin of black, if the basic color is brown. Belly light yellow toward head, changes to pink toward the tail.

A member of the Whipsnake family of the western states. A nervous and agile snake, feeding on lizards, frogs and small mammals.

Range: California and Lower California.

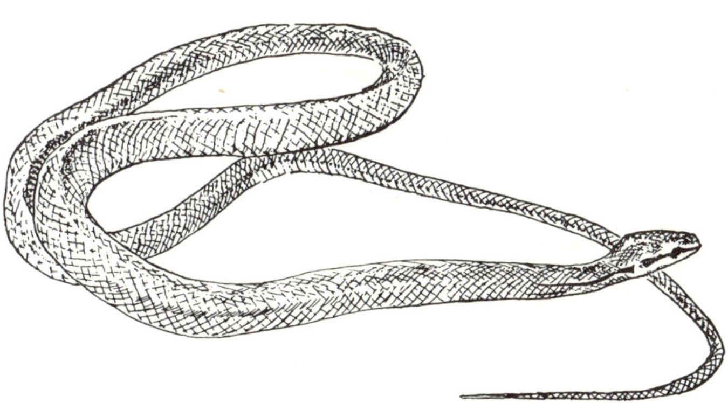

● WEST INDIAN RACER

Alsophis rufiventris

Average 3½ feet; largest 5 feet; non-poisonous.

Identified by the black stripe running from the tip of the nose to the after end of the neck. Usually light yellow or light brown.

A member of the rat-chasing family of snakes, although not as large and full bodied as North American snakes of the same type. Lives mostly on the ground and is at home in sandy or rocky soil.

Range: Southerly West Indies.

Hog Nosed Snakes

● EASTERN HOGNOSED SNAKE

Heterodon platyrhinos

Also called SPREADING-ADDER, PUFF-AD-DER, HISSING-ADDER, BLOW-SNAKE, or BLOW-ING-VIPER.

Average size 2 feet; maximum length 4½ feet; harmless.

Color variable. Ground color may be gray, yellow, brown, or tan. Usually large spots or blotches are present; these may be black, brown, gray, or reddish. Some specimens are entirely black, and a few are uniform blue-green.

This snake is absolutely harmless and cannot be made to bite. When disturbed, will hiss loudly and spread the neck widely, pretending to strike. The performance is mere bluff; and if further disturbed, the snake will flop over on its back and "play dead".

Range: New Hampshire and Minnesota southward through Florida and Texas.

● TEXAS PATCH-NOSED SNAKE

Salvadora grahamiae lineata

Average size 30 inches; largest 4 feet, 19 inches; non-poisonous.

Identified by a patch which appears to be stuck on the nose, possibly for burrowing. Usually striped brown and yellow, distinguishing them from the Leaf-nosed Snakes which are spotted. Feeds mostly on lizards.

Inhabiting the western desert and mountain country of United States. Quite active, can move with almost the rapidity of Racers.

● SOUTHERN HOGNOSED SNAKE *Heteron sinus*

Also called SPREADHEAD; BLOW SNAKE; PUFF ADDER; HISSING ADDER.

Average length 2 feet; largest 3½ feet; non-poisonous.

Distinguished and recognized by sharply upturned nose.

The defensive behavior of this snake furnishes the name and description. Usually when cornered will hold ground with the head inflating to twice normal size. Then a loud hiss is emitted with occasional strike, mouth widely opened. This failing to drive an enemy away, the snake will go into a fit and writhe on the ground; belly up, feigning death. Likes sandy soil; feeds on toads.

The snout is shovel-shaped for help in burrowing.

Range: North Carolina to Central Florida.

● WESTERN HOGNOSED SNAKE

Heterodon nasicus

Average size 3 feet; largest 38 inches.

Pale brown, yellow or gray with coarse irregular blotches on the back. Markings vary in all manner of designs. Principally identified by the snout. This is more pronounced than in other species.

Absolutely harmless, so much so it cannot be induced to bite, even though a finger is forced into the mouth. However, they put up the most terrifying show of viciousness ever seen by any reptile. This includes flattening the neck, loud hissing, vibrating the tail and repeated strikes toward the disturbing person. The tell-tale part of the act is that the snake does all this with the mouth closed.

Range: Texas and Arizona.

King Snakes

● **EASTERN KING SNAKE**   *Lampropeltis g. getulus*

Also called CHAIN SNAKE.

Average size 38 inches; largest 5 feet, 9 inches; harmless.

A shiny black snake with yellow cross bands that fork on the sides forming a chain-like pattern. Belly is black with white markings.

One of the best known snakes in the United States, especially in the pine tree belts. They like dry land, but are not necessarily confined to that terrain, and have been observed to have aquatic tendencies.

In captivity they are good natured, but sometimes they can cause alarm when they demonstrate their constricting ability by tightening a coil about the arm or hand. They do feed on poisonous snakes and destroy them extensively; however, they are not enemies, but are immune to Rattlesnake poison.

● **CALIFORNIA KING SNAKE**

Lampropeltis g. californiae.

Average length 40 inches; largest 4 feet, 2 inches; non-poisonous.

Glossy black with white rings which widen on the belly.

Noted for the unusual color pattern, which is entirely different from all other snakes of their habitat. This is one of the most common snakes of the Lower California area. Usually travels in daylight and does not like the desert or mountains.

Like other King Snakes they kill and eat Rattlesnakes, although they are notorious for robbing birds' nests.

Range: Southern Oregon, south through California and east to Nevada, and to Arizona.

● **ARIZONA KING SNAKE**

Lampropeltis p. pyromelana

Average size 24 inches; largest 41 inches; non-poisonous.

Series of white or cream color rings separated by black which is divided by red. The black fades away on the sides, rings are continuous around the belly. Light colored snout.

Prefer pine forests and high land. Not known to inhabit the desert or arid areas.

Range: From Arizona through Mexico.

● **BOYLE'S KING SNAKE**   *Lampropeltis g. boyli*

Average size 28 inches; largest on record 32½ inches; non-poisonous.

Black or sometimes brown with white or yellow crossbands, narrow on the back and wider at the sides. Head is dark, except snout, which is of a paler hue.

A smaller member of the King Snake family found in the West. Has the same characteristics of attacking other snakes and of being cannibalistic by nature. Will engage a Rattlesnake and kill it, when they meet.

Range: Found in Arizona and Lower California.

● S. FLORIDA KING SNAKE

Lampropeltis getulus brooksi

Average size 40 inches; largest 5 feet, 6 inches; non-poisonous, but they do bite.

Dull yellow, with a touch of brown on each scale. No discernible pattern of color.

The tropical variety of King Snake is found in the warm and humid areas of the Everglades; mostly on high sandy soil. While most King Snakes are supposed to be dry land reptiles, this Floridian sometimes takes to water.

When captured, will bite if possible, although there is no poison injection.

Range: Only seen in Collier, Glades and Monroe Counties, Florida.

● SHORT-TAILED SNAKE   *Stilosoma extenuatum*

Average size 18 inches; largest 24 inches; non-poisonous.

Slender snake with short tail. Silvery-gray with dark brown blotches. Sometimes spaces between the spots are reddish or yellowish.

A rare burrowing snake, usually found on high pine land or scrub. Does not appear to fear humans and will become enraged at rough handling, vibrating its stubby tail.

Range: Only known in Central part of Florida.

● CALIFORNIA LYRE SNAKE

Trimorphodon vandenburghi

Average length 24 inches; largest 30 inches; non-poisonous.

Blotched black and yellow.

A rear-fanged snake that kills small lizards but is harmless to man. Fairly rare snake.

Range: Found in the American southwest.

● ARIZONA LYRE SNAKE *Trimorphodon lyrophanes*

Average size 36 inches; largest 40 inches; slightly poisonous.

Each blotch on back is split by a white cross-line. Pattern on head looks like a lyre.

A broad-headed snake, with cat-like eyes, and grooved fangs in back of upper jaw. Will bite when cornered. Has poison sufficient to numb small animals.

Range: Found in Western Arizona, southward to Sonora and Lower California.

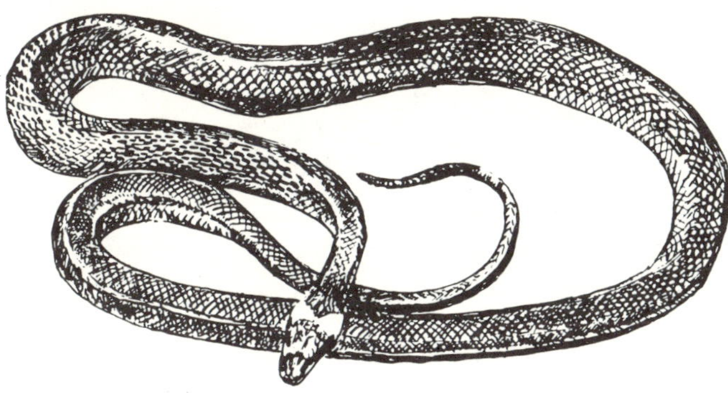

● WATER SNAKE
Natrix natrix

Average size 26 inches; largest 40 inches; non-poisonous.

Olive-gray with rows of small black spots. Has a broad yellow or white collar.

Feeds on frogs and toads and lives most of life in the water. Plays dead when cornered. Like most of the Garter Snakes can discharge foul smelling but harmless secretion, when threatened.

Range: Central Europe, western Asia and Algeria.

● TWO-STRIPED GARTER SNAKE
Thamnophis couchi hammondi

Also called BROWN'S GARTER SNAKE.

Average size 24 inches; largest 38 inches non-poisonous.

Brown basic color with lateral stripes of yellow. Four rows of alternate black spots. Belly pinkish.

A Garter Snake is usually found near the water. Prefers streams with rocky beds. When attempt is made to capture one, it usually dives in the water and hides under a rock. Feeds on frogs.

Range: Found in California, principally in southern part.

● CROWNED SNAKE
Tantilla coronata

Average length 9 inches; largest 13 inches; non-poisonous.

Black-headed and with a light band across the neck.

A small and secretive snake, usually found under stones and logs. Most abundant under plants and tree branches lying on the ground. Is a burrowing type.

Range: Coastal plains, Atlantic and Gulf of Mexico as far west as Louisiana and north up the Mississippi Valley to Kentucky.

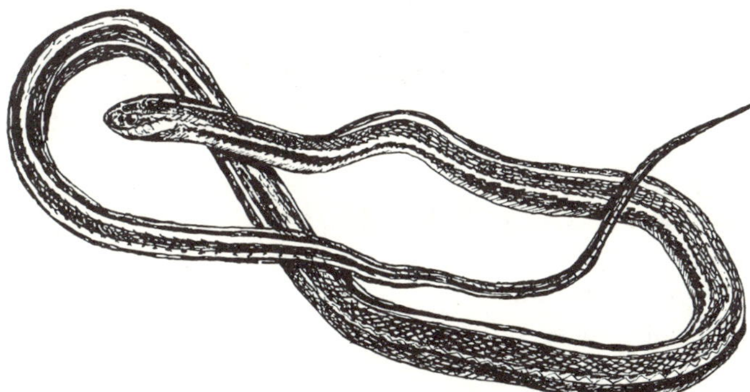

● WESTERN RIBBON SNAKE
Thamnophis proximus

Average size 2 feet; largest 4 feet; non-poisonous.

Body is marked with three vividly defined stripes on a dark brown or black background. The stripe on the back is always different in shade from that on the sides. Usually the back stripe is orange-yellow, while on the sides it is greenish-yellow. Belly greenish-white.

Live on a diet of frogs and fish. Like to gather in clusters on branches. When food appears, they break up as if a bomb had exploded. Are aquatic.

Range: Central states, Mississippi Valley, including Indiana and Illinois, and thence south right through to Central America.

● SOUTHERN RIBBON SNAKE
Thamnophis sauritis sackeni

Also called OSTEN-SACKEN'S RIBBON SNAKE.

Average size 16 inches; largest 22 inches; harmless.

Dark brown, green or olive above, with bright yellow stripe on each side. Yellow streak on head, or neck.

An aquatic type of the Ribbon Snake family. Frequently seen on branches of bushes, in the sun, especially overhanging the water. They drop in when alarmed.

Range: Found in Florida; also South Carolina and Georgia.

Garter Snakes

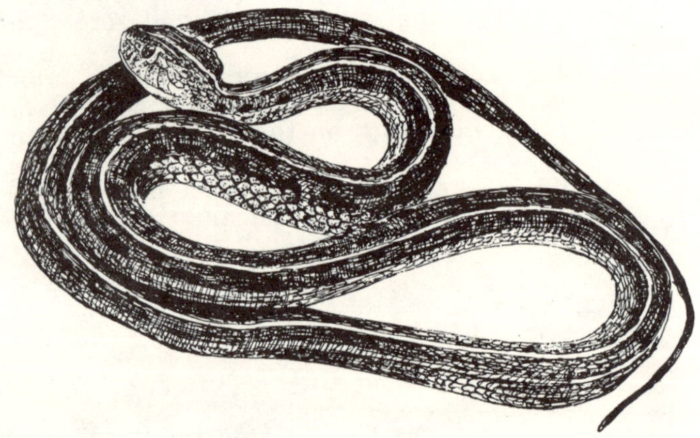

● GRAY GARTER SNAKE

Thamnophis ordinoides vagrans

Average size 25 inches; largest 28 inches; non-poisonous.

Greenish-gray or yellowish above, with narrow yellow stripe on the back and indistinct stripe on sides. Two rows of rounded black spots on the forward part of body; gray below, marbled with black.

This small docile snake is very common throughout the western states. While not a "water snake", it will go into the water in pursuit of food or to escape.

Range: Found throughout the western United States from Washington to California.

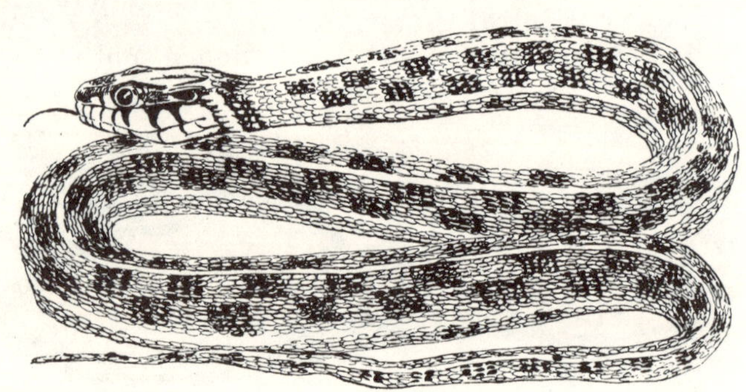

● CHECKERED GARTER SNAKE

Thamnophis marcianus

Average size 18 inches; largest 26 inches; non-poisonous.

Ground color light brown. Belly pale. Three yellow stripes, the central one more distinct and of brighter hue. Squarish black blotches between the mid and lateral stripes give it a checkerboard appearance.

Unlike most Garter Snakes, this one is more active at night.

Range: Kansas, Oklahoma & Texas into California.

● BUTLER'S GARTER SNAKE

Thamnophis butleri

Also called SMALL-HEADED GARTER SNAKE.

Average size 18 inches; largest 25 inches; non-poisonous.

Olive to brownish with three yellow or orange stripes. Likes grassy areas near water. Two other small Garter Snakes, the Mexican and the Short-heads, are so similar as to be distinguished only by range or scale count.

Inhabits grassy and bushy terrain.

Range: Eastern United States and west in the National Parks.

● CALIFORNIA GARTER SNAKE

Thamnophis ordinoides elegans

Also called PACIFIC COAST GARTER SNAKE.

Average size 18 inches; largest 30 inches; non-poisonous.

Particularly distinct central stripe is more vivid yellow than lateral ones. Body brownish with faint spots.

Range: California and Western Nevada.

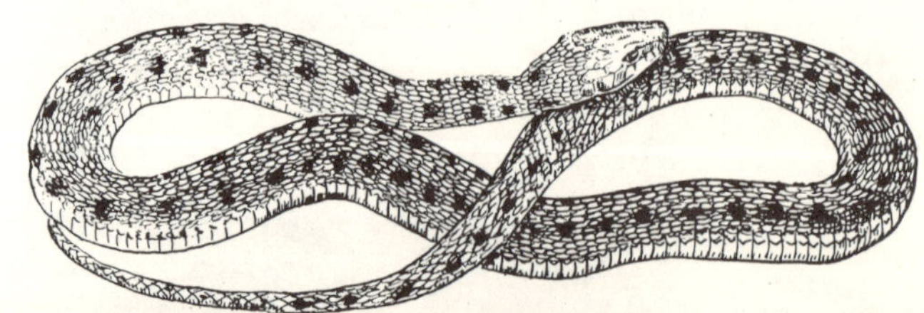

●SPOTTED GARTER SNAKE

Thamnophis sirtalis ordinatus

Average size 24 inches; largest 30 inches; non-poisonous.

Green to blackish-brown with rows of square blackish spots. There are no stripes.

Range: Mostly found in New England States. A sub-species of common Garter Snake.

Small Sand Snakes

● BANDED SAND SNAKE

Chilomeniscus cinctus

Average size 8 inches; largest 10; harmless.
Yellow, sometimes red with dark brown or black bands forming complete rings around the body. Belly whitish.

A small desert snake with a shovel-nose snout which is adapted to burrowing in loose sand. Spends most of the day buried and comes out at night.
Range: Western deserts, California, Arizona.

● WESTERN INDIGO SNAKE

Drymarchon corais

Also called TROPICAL INDIGO SNAKE.
Average size 5 feet; largest 7 feet, 9 inches; harmless. General color is brown; blackish toward tail. South American, branch of Indigo family.

One of the largest non-poisonous snakes and a favorite with snake charmers due to their docility and ease of feeding in captivity. Get along well in company of humans. Like the Indigo Snake, they like high and dry land and make use of burrows dug by gophers for their homes.
Range: Texas to South America.

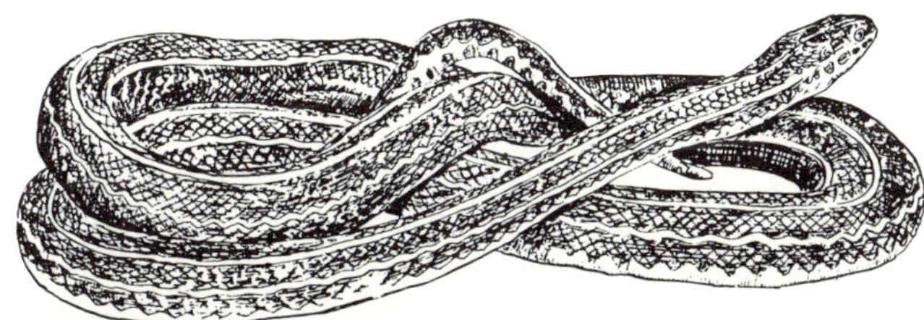

● RAINBOW SNAKE

Abastor erythrogrammus

Average size 4 feet; largest unknown; harmless.
Basic color bluish-black, with three longitudinal red stripes and a yellow stripe on the sides. Belly red, with double row of dark brown spots.
A fairly rare snake, of which not much is known. Burrowing type, only occasionally seen above ground. A brilliantly colored snake; has a tail spine like the Mud Snake.
Range: Maryland to Florida and Alabama.

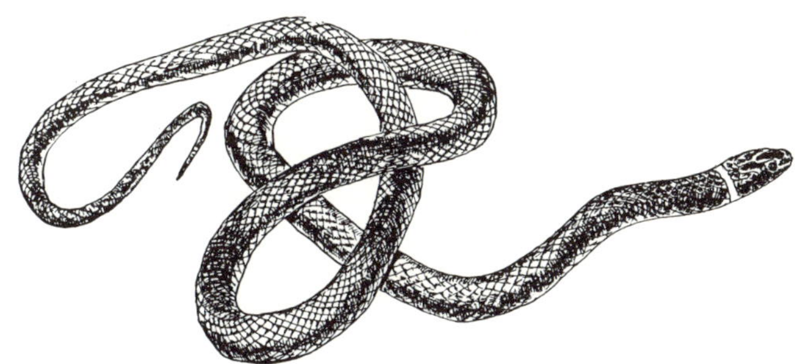

● PACIFIC RINGNECKED SNAKE

Diadophis punctatus amamilis

Average size 16 inches; largest 24 inches; harmless. Basic color is bluish or gray, with yellow neck ring standing out boldly. Belly is brilliant yellow or coral-red. If disturbed, it coils, hiding its head, and raising its tail to display bright underside.

Live in the wooded area of the United States West Coast. Do not care for the hot valleys. Dine mostly on tree frogs and spend a great deal of time coiled on stones. Secretive by nature.

Three members of this clan, all similar, are found in the U. S., divided roughly into the western, the southwestern and the eastern areas.

● SPOTTED NIGHT SNAKE

Hypsiglena torquata orchorhyncha

Average size 12 inches; largest 16 inches; non-poisonous.

Basic color gray or yellowish, with a mid-back row of darker spots, and a second row of smaller dots on the side.

Although not a fanged and poisonous snake, the saliva of this reptile is poisonous and if introduced into cuts or bruises, will cause a dangerous sore. This is used by the snake to subdue lizards.
Lives in rocky terrain and travels only at night.
Range: Pacific Coast and Great Plains.

Burrowing Snakes

● SMOOTH EARTH SNAKE *Virginia valeriae*

Average size 8 inches; largest 12 inches non-poisonous.

Chestnut or dirty brown—smooth scales. Secretive; found hiding under stones or trash. There are three subspecies common to different areas of the U. S.

Range: New Jersey to Texas.

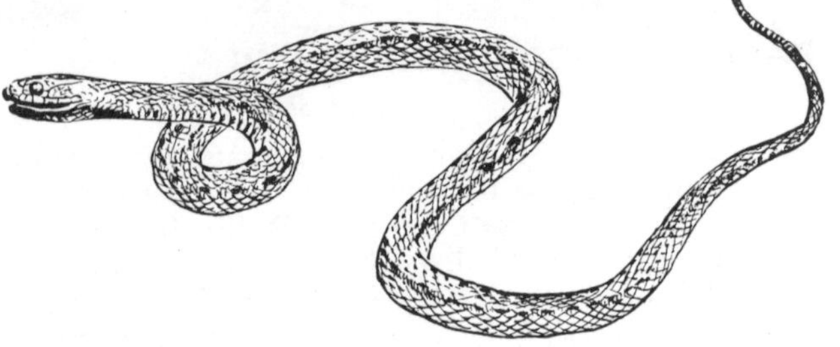

● DeKAY'S SNAKE *Storeria dekayi*

Also called BROWN SNAKE.

Average size 10 inches; largest 17 inches; harmless. General color is brown with clay-colored stripe down the middle of the back, bordered by small black dots.

Small urban dweller. A common snake often found congregated in great numbers under trash piles or lumber. There are four subspecies, all rather similar, in various areas from Maine to Texas.

● RUBBER BOA *Charina bottae*

Also called BALL SNAKE.

Average size 18 inches; largest 30 inches, according to Ditmar; harmless. Grayish to yellowish, sometimes greenish-brown. Stubby tail.

A burrowing snake, preferring damp environment. The rubbery appearance of body gives it the name. Very inoffensive, never attempting to bite or defend itself. When cornered, will often roll into a ball. Range: California to Utah.

● BROWN SAND BOA *Eryx johni*

Also called INDIAN BOA, TWO-HEADED SNAKE.

Average size 2 feet; largest 30 inches, according to Ditmar; harmless. Solid brown with faintly, almost indiscernible markings.

The tail of this burrowing snake ends so abruptly it looks like another head. This is taken advantage of by the Indian fakirs, who paint a mouth and eyes on the tail and exhibit as a reptile with two heads. They explain that while one head sleeps, the other watches.   Found in India.

● MOLE SNAKE *Lampropeltis calligaster rhombomaculata*

Also called BROWN KING SNAKE.

Average size 3 feet; largest 3 feet 9 inches; non-poisonous.

This is the burrowing member of the King Snake family—often turned up in plowing—occasionally found in the open and in brush.

Basic color light brown with a number of rounded, reddish-brown blotches edged in black; changes to yellowish toward the belly, checked with dark brown.

Range: From Maryland south to Central Florida and west to Tennessee and Mississippi.

Burrowing Snakes

● LONG-NOSED SNAKE

Rhinocheilus lecontei

Average size 24 inches; largest on record 37 inches; harmless.

A speckled-looking snake, having a series of large black or brown blotches down the back, with groups of yellow dots down the sides; or rather black dots on yellow ground color. Belly yellow or white, usually with a few black spots.

A burrowing snake with long snout, designed to dig into loose, sandy soil. Seldom seen in forest or desert, but in between, in sparse growth, sandy soil, it is most common. A nocturnal snake and rarely seen in daylight. Considered a constrictor by some scientists.

Range: Kansas, south through Texas and west to California.

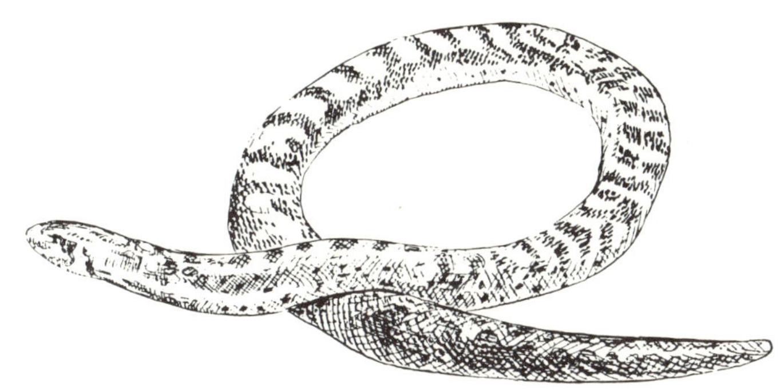

● EGYPTIAN SAND BOA

Eryx jaculus

Average size 18 inches; largest 24 inches; harmless.

Prettily marked with variegated saddles on the back and salt and pepper markings along the side, resembling the sand in which much time is spent.

Another of the burrowing snakes of the Boa family. Like the others, has a blunt head and tail. Prefers hot sands of the desert and likes temperatures over the 100 degree mark.

Range: North African and Central Asia.

● MOUNTAIN PATCH-NOSED SNAKE

Salvadora g. grahamiae

Also called FLAT-NOSED SNAKE.

Average size 20 inches; largest 30 inches; harmless.

Identified by wide yellow band down the back, bordered on each side by dark brown band. Sides are greenish or pale brown; belly, yellow.

Range: Fairly abundant in the United States, mostly western Texas and southward into Mexico. Rarely seen, due to nocturnal habits.

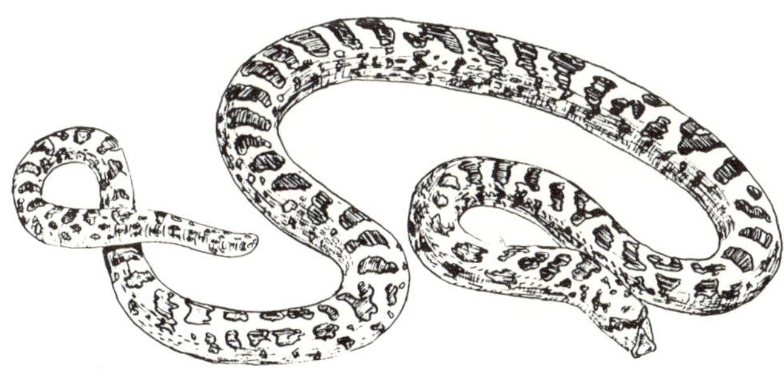

● DESERT LEAF-NOSED SNAKE

Phyllorhynchus decurtatus perkinsi

Average size 15 inches; largest on record 19½ inches; non-poisonous.

Identified by the patch or appendage on nose in the shape of a leaf. Dark blotches on a brownish basic color.

A night-roving desert snake which for a long time was thought to be very rare, until the automobile came along. Now it is known to be one of the commonest snakes of the Southwest. Many hundreds are seen on highways at night in automobile headlights.

Range: Mostly in Arizona and Southern California.

Water Snakes

● **DIAMOND-BACKED WATER SNAKE**
Natrix r. rhombifera

Average size 4 feet, 6 inches, according to Dismars; non-poisonous.

Olive color with narrow chain of black markings enclosing diamond-shaped areas of ground color. Abdomen is yellow.

This snake has a well defined head with large lip plates and protruding lips. Eyes are well forward.

Vicious looking and vicious acting, the Diamond-back, although not poisonous gives the appearance of being venomous. Will strike at anything which gets close.

Range: Illinois to Texas and Mississippi valley.

● **BLOTCHED WATER SNAKE**
Natrix erythrogaster transversa

Average size 28 inches; largest 36 inches; non-poisonous.

Brown above with a series of large blotches on the back, separated by narrow lines of ground color. The belly is yellow, clouded with brown.

Lives in swamps and on riverbanks. A smaller species of water snake feeding on fish and small lizards.

Range: Westerly from Louisiana to Mexico.

● **TESSELLATED SNAKE**
Natrix tessellata

Average size 24 inches; largest 36 inches; non-poisonous.

Distinguished by the rows of small spots arranged in checkerboard pattern. The spots are black on a basic yellow color, making a striking contrast.

A harmless and sought after snake in the Gypsy camps of Europe. The skin makes beautiful belts and ornaments. They tame easily and like human companionship. Feed on small frogs.

Range: Italy, Switzerland and Bohemia.

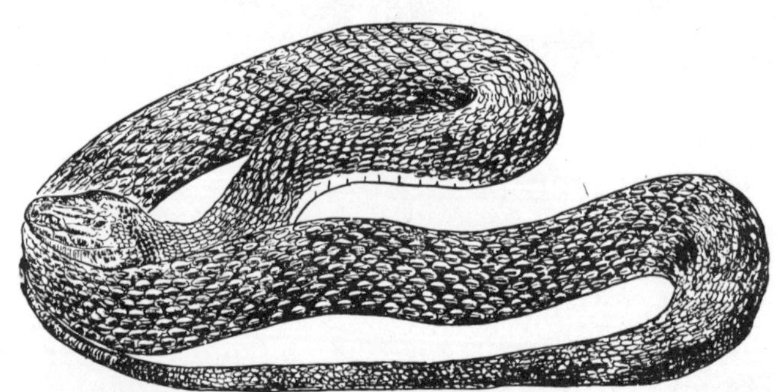

● **GREEN WATER SNAKE**
Natrix cyclopion

Average size 3 feet; largest 4 feet, 6 inches, according to Ditmars; non-poisonous.

Dark-green with numerous black bands across the back; lips are yellow; belly is yellow with tinge of gray upon the edge of the plates.

An ugly and formidable looking water snake, one of the largest. Close cousin to the Diamondback Water Snake, although not so vicious in temperament. Like most water snakes, prefers to climb trees.

Range: Found throughout the Gulf states and particularly in Florida where the largest specimens have been collected.

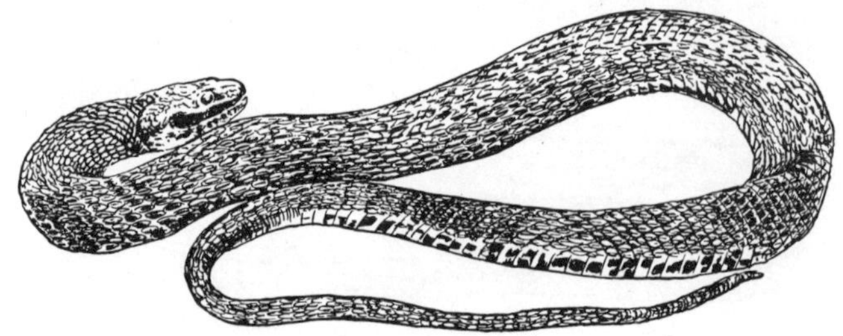

● **BROWN WATER SNAKE**
Natrix taxispilota

Also called WATER RATTLE; WATER PILOT.

Average size 3 feet; largest 5 feet, according to Ditmars; non-poisonous.

Rusty-brown with a series of black or dark-brown blotches on the back, square in shape. Belly is yellow, profusely blotched with brown.

This is the largest of the water snakes and one of the ugliest looking of American snakes. Has a mean disposition and will coil and strike on the order of a poisonous snake when cornered.

Can be seen stretched on Palmetto bushes near the water. Will jump at the slightest sound.

Range: From the Potomac River south to Florida and particularly abundant in the Georgia swamps and Florida Everglades.

Water Snakes

● NORTHERN WATER SNAKE   *Natrix s. sipedon*

Also called BANDED WATER SNAKE.

Average length 3 feet; largest 4 feet, 6 inches caught in New York State; non-poisonous.

Yellowish with dark blotches on sides and back. Halfmoon markings on belly scales.

Feeds on non-game fish mostly in slow moving rivers or lakes. Sometimes confused with a Moccasin, although not poisonous and usually considered a scavenger of the waters.

Range: Eastern United States.

● BANDED WATER SNAKE   *Natrix s. fasciatia*

Also called FALSE MOCCASIN.

Average 3 feet; largest 4 feet; non-poisonous.

Pale brownish ground color, tending to become red on sides. Pattern of dark bands across back. Belly is yellowish-white.

This is the snake most commonly confused with a poisonous Moccasin. The difference is that this harmless snake is more slender and a definite proof is the red spots on the belly. Under surface of a poisonous snake is straw color with possible black spots, but never red spots. The poisonous snake has a large pit between the eye and nostril which is not present in a harmless snake.

Fish-eating and rather abundant in southern waters, including large numbers in Florida.

Range: Up Mississippi valley to Indiana and west to Nebraska.

● RED-BELLIED WATER SNAKE
Natrix e. erythrogaster

Also called COPPER-BELLIED MOCCASIN.

Average size 30 inches; largest 4 feet; non-poisonous.

Rusty-brown above; brick-red on belly.

Has the same habits as a Common Water Snake, but is more docile. In captivity submits to handling and generally appears to like fondling.

Found in swamps, river banks and all Southern waterways.

Range: Atlantic Coast from Virginia to Florida.

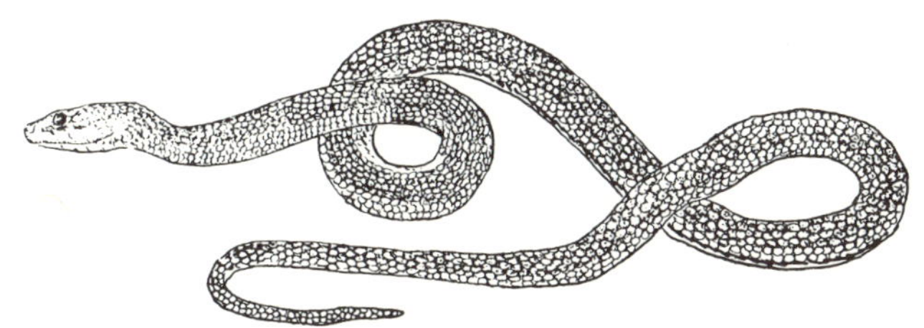

● GRAHAM'S WATER SNAKE   *Regina grahami*

Average size 25 inches; largest 36 inches; non-poisonous.

Dark brown on back with distinct pale band down center. Broad band of yellow on each side.

An agile and timid species of water snake, found mostly in streams and lakes of fairly clear water. Quite secretive and usually hidden under bark or logs on river bank.

Range: Throughout Mississippi and Missouri River valleys.

Swamp and Mud Snakes

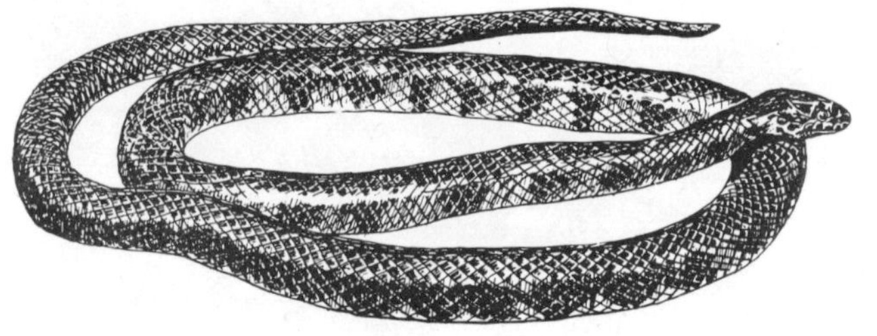

● **EASTERN MUD SNAKE** *Farancia abacura abacura*

Also called HORN SNAKE; STINGING SNAKE.

Average length 4 feet; largest on record 6 feet according to Ditmars.

Shiny, heavy body with short and abruptly tapering tail which has a sharp spine in the end. Basic color is black or bluish-black with a number of red markings, triangular shape, on sides; red belly.

Lives in the swamplands of the South and usually burrows in the river banks. The "Stinging Snake" name and legend come from a spine in its tail. This the snake presses into the hand of a captor. Actually there is no poison or stinging ability. Another myth is its alleged ability to put its tail in its mouth, forming a hoop, then roll at great speed.

Range: Virginia to Florida, west to Alabama.

● **BLACK SWAMP SNAKE** *Seminatrix pygaea*

Also called RED-BELLIED MUD SNAKE.

Average size 12 inches; largest 17 inches; non-poisonous.

Uniform black with red belly. Conspicuous narrow black bar extends in from either end of each belly plate. Somewhat resemble teeth of a comb.

Found around the edge of ponds and where there is considerable growth. Can be located by rolling up a batch of Hyacinth in shallow water. Feeds mostly on fishes.

Range: North Carolina through Florida.

● **FLAT-TAILED WATER SNAKE**
Natrix s. compressicauda

Also called MANGROVE WATER SNAKE.

Average 2 feet; largest 3 feet, 2 inches.

Greenish-gray, with irregular cross bars. Head is darker than body; lower surface is dark gray with central row of yellow dots; unique in having a vertically compressed tail.

Usually found in coastal swamps where fresh and salt water mix. Likes mangrove thickets and salt marshes. Considered on the timid side. Lives on fish. Very efficient swimmer. Non-poisonous.

Range: Coastal regions of South Florida only.

● **KIRTLAND'S WATER SNAKE** *Natrix kirtlandi*

Average size 15 inches; longest on record, 21 inches; non-poisonous.

Checkered. Pattern of four rows of black blotches on ground color of light brown to gray. Belly bright red, with a row of conspicuous black spots.

When alarmed, snake makes ineffectual strikes, but is never known to bite when handled.

Most common in swampy areas, not in streams or ponds.

Range: From Wisconsin to New Jersey.

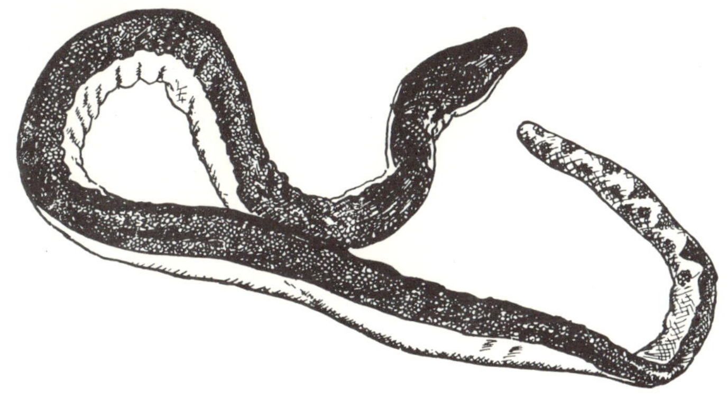

● YELLOWBELLIED SEASNAKE

Pelamis platurus

Average size 2 feet; largest 3 feet; poisonous. Identified by yellow belly, and dark back. Give the appearance of being put together in two parts. Curious pattern of triangles on the rudder-like tail.

A marine serpent, spending all the time in the ocean and one of several of the tropical Pacific. They often get entangled in fishermen's nets to their great dismay. Although not always fatally poisonous, their bite leaves a bad infection which often has fatal results.

Range: Pacific Ocean, principally off Mexico.

● RINGED SEASNAKE

Laticauda colubrina

Average length 3 feet; largest 5 feet; dangerously poisonous.

Distinguished by the small size head in comparison to the body. Colors vary and the snake is often covered with a green moss-like coat.

This is a salt water snake that bites—and fatally, the fishermen of the Pacific who catch it in their nets. They use their venom to paralyze fishes and eels for food and have a broad flat tail to aid in swimming.

Range: Indian and Pacific oceans.

● SMALLHEADED SEASNAKE

Microcephalophis gracilis

Average size 30 to 35 inches; largest 42 inches; poisonous.

Color grayish-yellow to olive with darker crossbands; head dark. As its name indicates, the anterior portion is very small compared to its oversized midsection. Probably an adaptation useful in poking into holes after eels—its favorite food. It has been known to bite humans; venom highly toxic.

Range: South Asian to Australian coastal waters.

● MANGROVE SNAKE

Boiga dendrophilus

Average size 4 feet; largest 6 feet; harmless.

Black basic color with white lips and white rings, widening at the belly. A row of eight markings vertically on line.

Usually found around the shore line in the Mangrove bushes of Pacific islands.

Range: Malaya to Philippines.

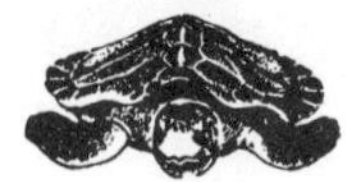

Common Turtles

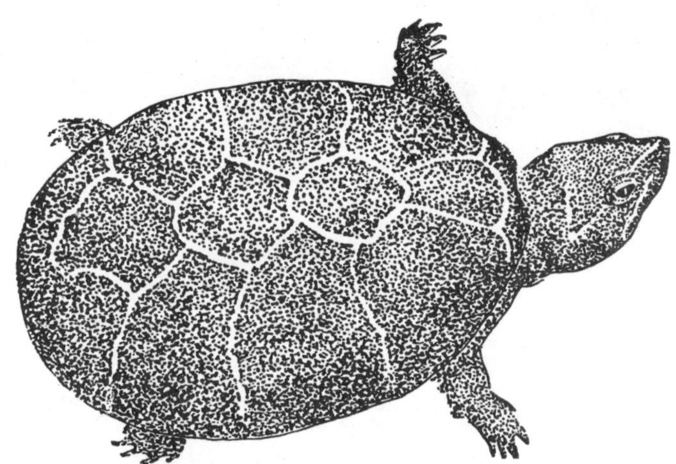

TURTLES have been around for two hundred million years. The dinosaurs were newcomers to them; they didn't last, but the turtles went on and on.

Some live on land, some in water, and some enjoy the best of both worlds.

While the whole family may properly be called turtles, three terms are used to group them according to life style. "Turtles" are aquatic or semi-aquatic, "terrapins" are semi-aquatic, while "tortoises" are the land-lubbers.

Bizarre creatures all; toothless reptiles with skeletons on the outside, the female sometimes grows to several times the size of her mate. Some lay hundreds of eggs at a time—some only one. They mature in 5 to 7 years—then sometimes go on to live to the ripe old age of 150 years.

Some are vicious, some make good pets. Some are prized as food. Some are "stinkers". Sizes range from midget to giant, and colors from drab to vivid.

Many are protected by law—and fortunate it is. Having let us share this planet for all these years. they must not be allowed to follow the dinosaur.

● **STINKPOT** *Sternotherus odoratus*

Also called STINKIN' JENNY.

Average size 5½ inches; largest 6 inches; harmless, though offensive, with a mean temper. Ferocious for size.

One of the musk turtle family; easily recognized by offensive smell. Dark brown carapace.

Found in ponds and sluggish streams of North America. Often with coating of green scum on back. Spends much time in the mud, hunting for fish eggs and tadpoles. Will scavenge dead fish or fowl.

Quite often they take a fisherman's hook and when the turtle and smell rises to the surface, a wise fisherman will cut the line—fast.

Range: Eastern United States.

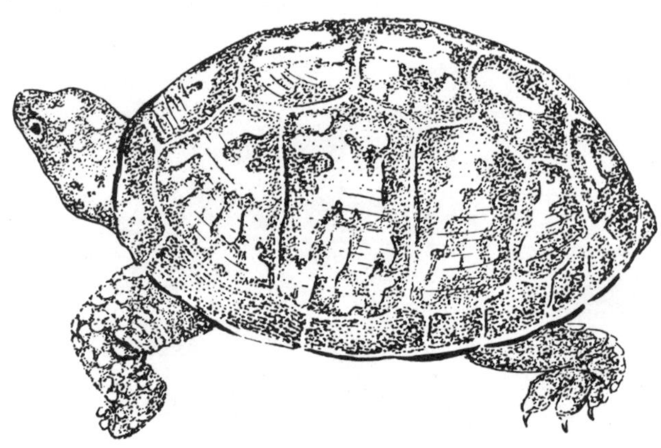

● **BOX TURTLE** *Terrapene carolina*

Average size 5 inches; largest 6½ inches; edible.

Has ability to withdraw head and legs into shell and close it to form a box. Mottled white and brown.

Lives in mud during hot summer months, comes out on land and lives on river banks in spring and fall. Has a very long life. Makes a good pet. Lays eggs in ground.

Several species, all fairly similar abound throughout eastern half of U. S.

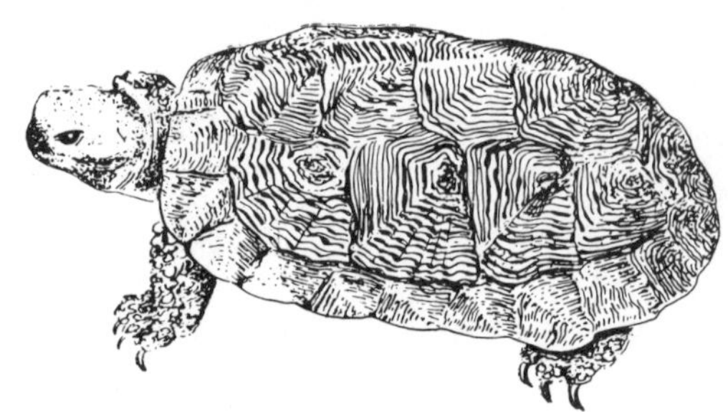

● **WOOD TURTLE** *Clemmys insculpta*

Average length 5 inches; largest 9 inches; edible, considered a delicacy.

Shell has sculptured appearance. Tail often as long as carapace. Has reddish legs.

Quite popular as a pet. Shy at first, but can be tamed to eating from the hand. Entirely harmless. Feed as much as they will eat. Consume small amount in winter. Should be fed daily in summer.

At one time were caught and sold for food commercially, but now protected in most states.

Range: Northwestern United States.

River Turtles

● EASTERN CHICKEN TURTLE
Deirochelys r. reticularia

Average size 7 inches; largest 9 inches. Edible, but small amount of meat hardly worth while.

Usually olive or dusky brown in color; plastron is immaculate yellow; head and neck, brown with longitudinal green stripes.

Usually found in ponds and lakes. A sociable but timid creature. They spend much time basking on logs in the sun. Often swim in groups. Unusually long neck distinguishes this species.

Found along the southern coastal regions from North Carolina to Texas.

● REEVE'S TURTLE
Chinemys reevesi

Average size 4 inches; largest 5 inches; harmless.

Uniform dull brown; silvery-white eyes, very sharp and piercing; belly, usually dark yellow.

An agile swimmer, preferring aquatic surroundings to the dryness of woodland. Feeds on fish, worms and grasses. Very timid. Will dive and hide at the slightest sound. Before surfacing will poke out the tip of nose and take a good look around with the two sharp eyes. A good pet for the home aquarium.

Range: China and Japan.

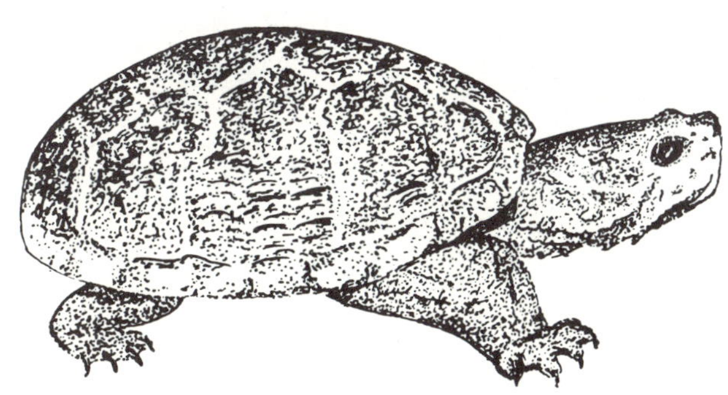

● MUD TURTLE
Kinosternon subrubrum

Average size 3 inches; largest 6 inches; harmless.

Top shell drab brown, sometimes with black edges on the shields.

Like the Musk Turtle, they emit an offensive odor, but to a lesser degree. Live in muddy water throughout the summer and leave for higher ground to burrow below the surface in winter. Feed on fish and insects. In captivity will eat chopped fish or meat.

Distributed throughout North America.

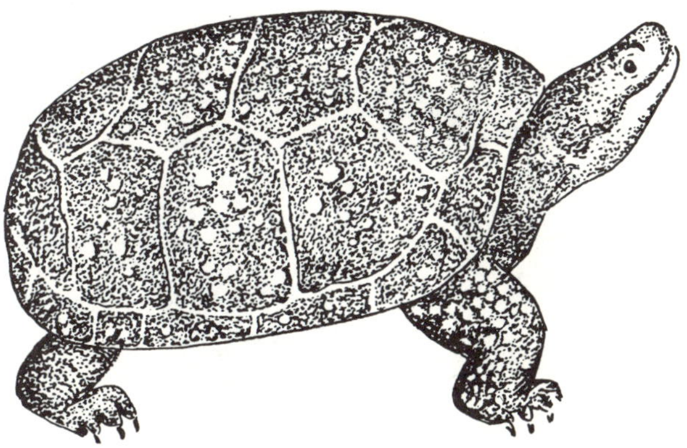

● BLANDING'S TURTLE
Emydoidea blandingi

Average size, 6 inches; largest 10 inches; harmless; no food value.

Distinguished by brilliant yellow chin; throat and domed shell covered with streaks and spots of yellow.

Essentially aquatic, although travels some portion of life on land. Feeds on snails and crayfish.

Range: Great Lakes area.

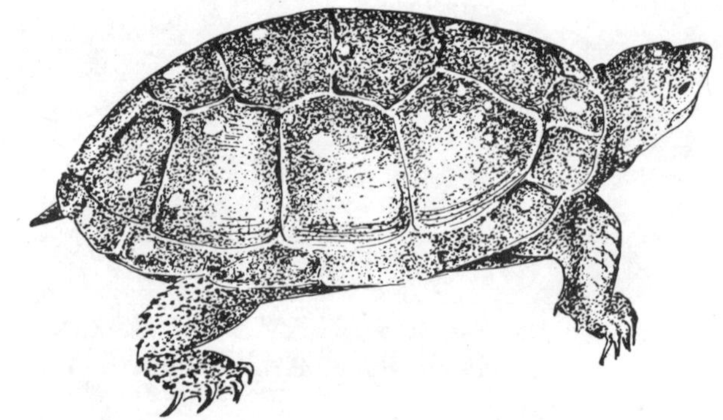

● SOUTH AMERICAN SNAKE-NECK TURTLE
Hydromeduso tecitifuro

Also called SIDE-NECK TURTLES.

Average size 6 inches; largest 8 inches; neck to 10 inches; harmless.

Identified by the serpentine neck, longer than the carpace.

An aquatic breed, at home ashore or afloat. Have the particuliar habit of folding up their neck in lateral curves. It is too long to pull into the shell as do other turtles. Feeds on grass and insects along river banks.

Range: Tropical South America.

● SPOTTED TURTLE
Clemmys guttata

Average size 3 inches; largest 5 inches.

Bright yellow spots on a black carapace.

A slow-moving small turtle that is never in a hurry. Chooses quiet, small streams and margins of pools and lakes. Makes a good little pet but must be given a place to hide-—will eat meat, fish and bits of lettuce.

Found throughout Eastern United States.

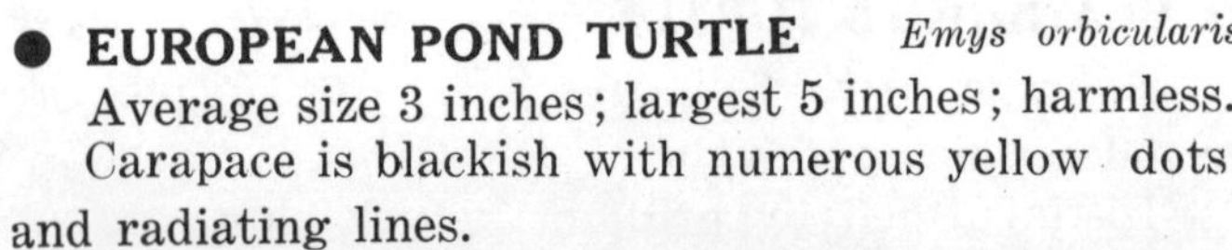

● EUROPEAN POND TURTLE
Emys orbicularis

Average size 3 inches; largest 5 inches; harmless.

Carapace is blackish with numerous yellow dots and radiating lines.

A river turtle which does come out on land somewhat. Eats under water and spends most of the time submerged. Prefers good fresh water. Eats grasses and fish. Usually found in the headwater ponds of creeks.

Range: Europe, Asia and northern Africa.

● AFRICAN MUD TURTLE
Pelusios derbianus

Average size 10 inches; largest 12 inches; harmless.

Upper shell uniform black or dingy brown. Head has numerous streaks and dots.

A water turtle which is never seen on land. Eats, sleeps and lives under the water. Can remain submerged for long periods of time. Eats fish, meat or grasses.

Range: Africa and Madagascar.

 # Soft Shelled Turtles 

● SPINY SOFT-SHELLED TURTLE

Trionyx spiniferus

Average size adult, 12 inches in diameter.

Adults are light olive-brown; breastplate is white; front edge of shell is armed with spines. Two light stripes down the head. Young have black circles on outer shell.

A bit more hardy than other soft shelled turtles.

Found in Mississippi to St. Lawrence and Great Lakes.

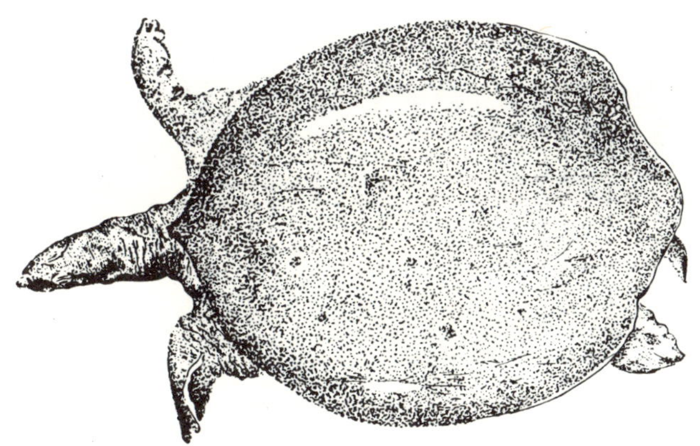

● SPINELESS SOFT-SHELLED TURTLE

Trionyx muticus

Average size 7 inches; largest 14 inches; edible.

Uniform pale brown or olive. They match the muddy river bottom.

A river turtle, feeding on fish in the muddy and slow moving rivers. Is sought for food by local fishermen in the Mississippi Valley.

Range: Mississippi Valley and eastward to Pennsylvania.

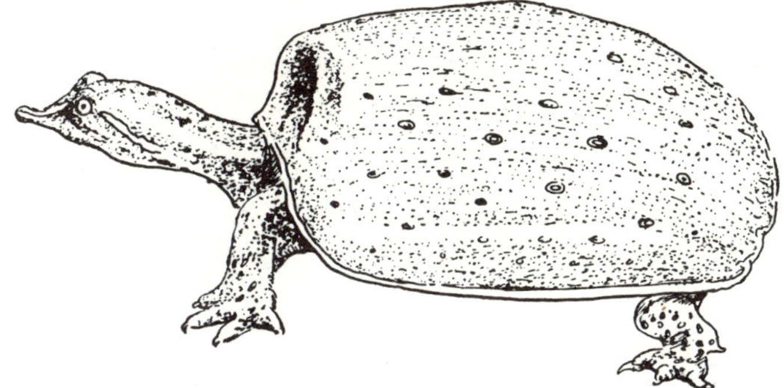

● GULF COAST SOFT-SHELLED TURTLE

Trionyx s. asper

Average length 2 inches.

Has light brown carapace covered with small black spots. Lines encircle the rear half of the carapace. The upper part of the carapace covered with tubercles.

Range: North Carolina to Mississippi.

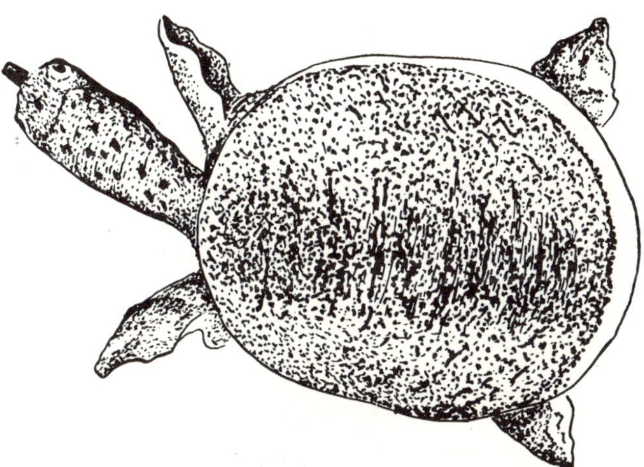

● FLORIDA SOFT-SHELLED TURTLE

Trionyx ferox

Average size 12 inches; largest 18 inches, and weighing 40 pounds. Harmless; edible.

Light olive-brown above and white below. Young mottled with black.

This is the largest of the American soft-shelled turtles. Found in lakes and rivers of the southeastern part of the United states.

Caught by hook and line, and a favorite food of many native Southerners. The smaller sizes are cooked whole after being cleaned and beheaded. Insides may be drawn through a hole cut in breastplate.

Never leaves the water on extended jaunts except to deposit eggs. Easily bruised on rocky shores. Can be kept in captivity. Tank should have sand bottom and a log or board for turtle style sunbathing.

Range: South Carolina, Georgia, Florida.

Queer and Ugly Turtles

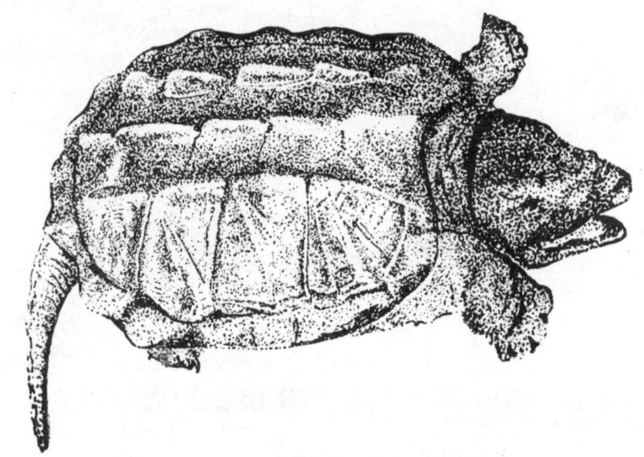

● ALLIGATOR SNAPPING TURTLE

Macrochelys temmincki

Adults grow to 3 feet, and weigh over 200 pounds. Dangerous when cornered.

Heavy, bony carapace. Large vicious mouth capable of biting off a man's hand. Dull yellow. Three rows of keels.

This is the largest, ugliest and most vicious turtle in North America. Called "Alligator Turtle" because of long tail. Captures fish for food by using "decoy" worms attached to the tongue. These are waved in the water to entice fish close enough for the snapping jaws to clamp down.

They travel on land as well as in the water.

Mostly inhabiting lower Mississippi River, also the Gulf States and around Florida to Suwannee River.

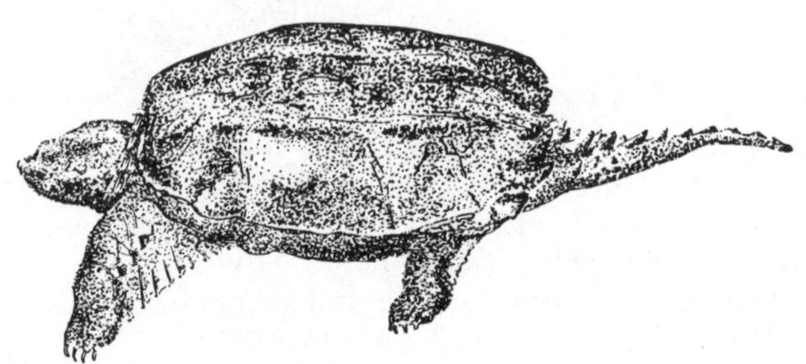

● SNAPPING TURTLE

Chelydra s. serpentina

Average size 12 inches; largest 2 feet across, weighing 60 pounds; edible, but dangerous, can bite off a finger.

Has a greenish coloration, often with moss clinging to back. Keeled tail.

Will attack and eat most anything. Feeds on grass and wading birds and fish. Has a long neck which darts out and snaps at anything in reach. Often captured and fed in captivity before butchering for food.

Range: Eastern part of United States.

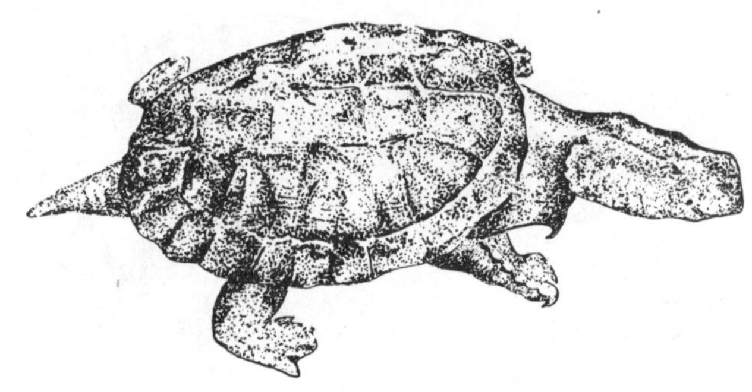

● MATAMATA TURTLE

Chelys fimbriata

Average size 24 inches; largest 3 feet; harmless. Resembles a log covered with rough bark, dark brown in color.

Spend a good part of their lives lying motionless in the water, resembling the background so much, that only an expert turtle hunter can detect their presence. Considered the queerest and ugliest of the reptile family.

Esteemed for food. Feed on frogs and tadpoles.

Range: Inhabit the muddy waters of the Amazon River.

● ALGERIAN TURTLE

Clemmys leprosa

Average size 6 inches; largest 9 inches; harmless. Smooth, flattened shell; somber colors, green above, yellow below.

The Latin name of this creature is inspired by the appearance of some specimens. They suffer a disease which looks like leprosy. Principal habitation is in pools that partially evaporate during the hot season and become stagnant. They eat fish, raw meat, earthworms or lettuce, which is consumed under water.

Found in Southern Spain, Portugal, Algeria and Morroco.

Deep Sea Turtles

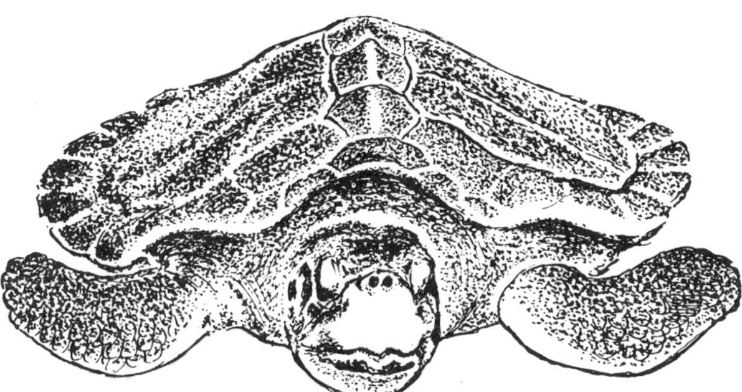

● RIDLEY SEA TURTLE
Lepidochelys

Also called BASTARD TURTLE.

Largest size known is 150 pounds; good food.

Resemble a Loggerhead Turtle. Usually only one claw on front flipper. Jaw is not beak-like. Has an underjaw to match upper, unusual in sea turtles. Might be considered a cross between a Loggerhead and a Green Turtle, which accounts for the fact that fisheries biologists have bestowed the title "Bastard".

Two species: One Atlantic, one Pacific.

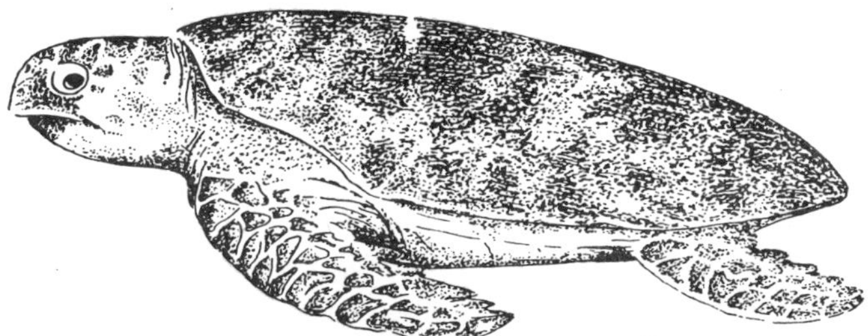

● LOGGERHEAD TURTLE
Caretta c. caretta

Also called LANTERNBACK TURTLE.

Average size 300 pounds; largest 800 pounds.

Is distinguished by having five or more pairs of shields on carapace. Limbs are paddle-shaped, each with two claws.

The Loggerhead is one of the oldest inhabitants of the sea. Ranges widely—inland waters to open sea throughout Atlantic, Carribean and Mediterranean. A common sight on the Florida Coasts.

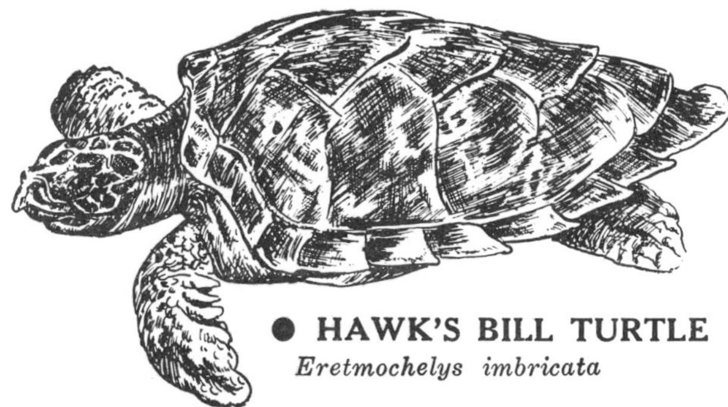

● HAWK'S BILL TURTLE
Eretmochelys imbricata

Average size 15 inches; largest 30 inches;

Identified by overlapping shields in the carpace. Upper mandible projects downward like a hawk's bill.

Smallest of the sea turtles, inhabits the Atlantic, Pacific, and Indian Oceans. Hunted extensively for their shells, which produce valuable "tortoise", used in jewelry making.

Range: Semitropical Seas.

● GREEN TURTLE
Chelonia mydas

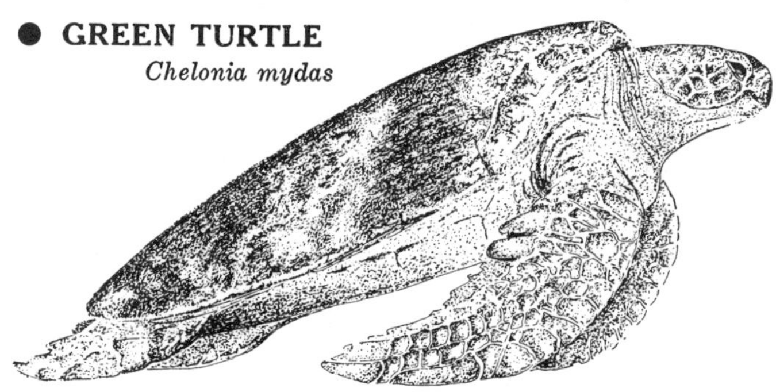

Average weight 120 pounds; largest on record 850 pounds; food value excellent.

Four shields on carpace. Do not overlap. Two claws on flipper. Carpace fused with vertebrae. Shields are translucent and take a high polish. Sold as tortoise shell.

They are found in comparatively shallow water, but not coral reefs. Most abundant in shoal water near low sandy beaches. They are herbivorous, feeding mostly upon marine grasses. Frequently come ashore to bask in sunshine.

Because they are hunted so diligently, the Green Turtle is becoming scarce. Today they are rarely given a chance to grow beyond 120 pounds. Fisheries experts agree that these turtles will be fished to extinction shortly unless protected with more stringent regulations.

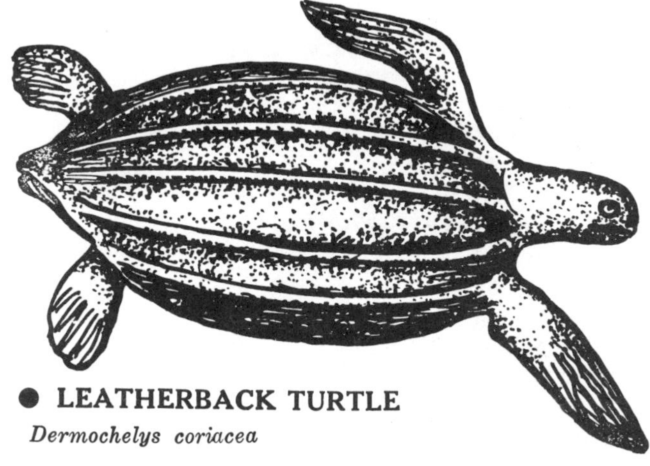

● LEATHERBACK TURTLE
Dermochelys coriacea

Also called TRUNK TURTLE or LUTH.

Average size 700 pounds; largest on record 1,450 pounds. Food value poor.

Has five pairs of shields. Shell is leathery and not fused with bony skeleton. Brown color, back mottled with yellow.

The largest of the turtles and most rare in coastal waters. Prefers deep water of Gulf or ocean. Although mostly tropical in habitat, are sometimes found in cold waters near the Arctic Ocean. Prefer a depth of 150 feet for normal living except when laying eggs. Lays eggs mostly in South America.

World Wide Turtles

● EASTERN SPUR-THIGHED TORTOISE
Testudo g. ibera

Also called IBERIAN TORTOISE.

Average size, 6 inches; largest, 9 inches; edible. Shell is pale, dirty yellow, sometimes brown, with a goodly number of black blotches.

A land-dwelling creature noted for very long life. One specimen has been recorded as 96 years old. Take to domesticity very well and many are living in gardens of urban dwellers. They answer to calls and feed on vegetation offered them.

Originate in North Africa and are known in Spain, Turkey, Roumania and southwest Asia.

● S. AMERICAN FOREST TURTLE
Geochelone denticulata

Average size 12 inches; largest 14 inches; edible; harmless.

Light pigment of carapace combined with pink eyes, give it an unusual appearance.

A rare breed of turtle, unlike any of other lands, is the Albino of the West Indies. Lack of pigment in a turtle shell is seldom encountered. Feeding as most Tortoise family members, on grass and roots, they are slow and sluggish and easily captured.

Range: Tropical South America and the West Indies Islands.

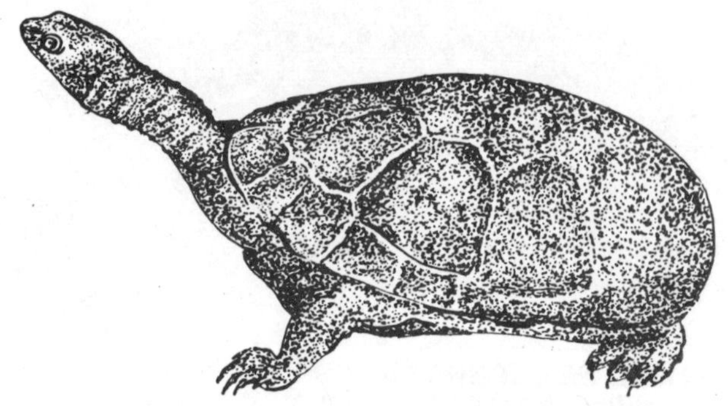

● AUSTRALIAN SNAKE-NECKED TURTLE
Chelodina longicollis

Average length 6 inches; largest 10 inches; edible.

Distinguished by long snake-like neck, which can weave from side to side like a snake about to strike.

Equally at home in water or on land. Does fine in captivity. Can be fattened up for food. The turtle always has a choice between land or water for daily comfort.

Range: Australia.

● HINGED-BACK TORTOISE
Kinixys

Average size 8 inches; largest 12 inches; edible.

Identified by smooth shell, upturned at the edges, somewhat resembling a German steel helmet used by infantrymen.

A land tortoise, roaming the grassy veldts and woods somewhat like the American Gopher Tortoise. Dig shallow holes for a home and become host to numerous rodents. Move slowly and deliberately. Natives prize the flesh for food. Has the ability to close the shell by moving the back instead of the lower plate, with soft cartilege in center acting as hinge.

Range: Tropical Africa.

Gopher Tortoise

● **GOPHER TORTOISE**　　*Gopherus polyphemus*

Average size 10 inches, weight 9 pounds; largest 12 inches, weight 16 pounds. Edible, considered a delicacy.

Dull yellowish blotch on each shield of carapace when young, this fades out to dull brown. The heart-shaped projection from shell is a spade to dig a hole.

Most friendly creature in the tortoise family. While no other tortoises or turtles visit him, the dens he burrows in the earth are usually full of guests. Owls, racoons, frogs, blacksnakes and rattlesnakes join the Gopher in his subterranean home.

Being a most accomplished digger, the Gopher builds by far the most livable underground hideouts. If unmolested, they could live for 100 years and furnish many homes for other members of the animal kingdom.

Range: Natives of Florida and Southern States of United States.

● **STARRED TORTOISE**　　*Geochelone elegans*

Average size 6 inches; largest 8 inches; edible.

Basic color is black with numerous yellow lines radiating. Under shell also black with yellow lines. Very high carapace.

Although this is a fairly common species of tortoise in some countries, they are difficult to find. Colors blend so well with the rocky countryside they inhabit, only the experienced can detect their presence.

Unusual is the process of egg-laying. The female deposits her eggs in a hole in the mud, which she has dug, then covers up with the dirt taken out, finishing off by beating down the area with her belly, so it is impossible to see a trace of the nest.

Range: India and Ceylon.

● **DESERT TORTOISE**　　*Gopherus agassizi*

Average size 12 inches; largest 14 inches; edible.

Similar to Florida Gopher, except smaller.

Western branch of the Gopher family, slightly darker and smaller. Likes sagebrush and cactus and moves about on the hot sand without discomfort. Burrows everywhere the ground is workable.

Range: Utah to Mexico.

● **TEXAS TORTOISE**　　*Gopherus belandieri*

Smallest of Gophers. Grow to about 8 inches.

Dull brown in color, no markings worthy of note.

An herbivorous tortoise, inhabiting dry, warm and sandy areas of the West. A close brother to the Southern Gopher Tortoise. They dig burrows with the attached spade on the lower shell and then become host to rattlesnakes and various lizards, all of which live amicably together.

Preferring tender shoots of plants, the Texas Tortoise has flesh relished by humans. They are considered a delicacy in many circles.

Range: Southern Texas and Northern Mexico.

Giant Tortoise

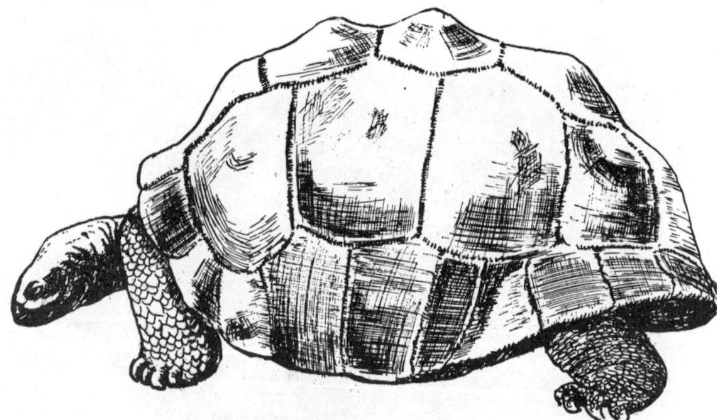

● **ELEPHANT TORTOISE** *Testudo elephantopus*

More commonly known as the GALAPAGOS TORTOISE.

Average 3 feet; largest 5 feet; weight over 500 lbs.

Huge, slow-moving vegetarians, native to the Galapagos Islands, (Galapagos means "Giant Turtle") they have been kept successfully in captivity around the world. Given a chance, they live to be a hundred and fifty years old; however, they have been hunted almost to extinction. In early days, the crews of sailing ships took them along for food on long journeys. They posed a puzzle to Darwin because they seemed to be land creatures originating on an island, with no apparent ancestor on the mainland.

Range: Found only on Galapagos Islands.

● **SOUTH ALBEMARLE TORTOISE**

Geochelone e elephantopus

One of the more than a dozen subspecies of the Galapagos giants which inhabit, respectively, the same number of isolated islands. All are similar, but each has some slight distinguishing characteristic. Some have been transplanted halfway around the world, have become citizens of the Seychelles Islands and are thriving under government protection.

Found in Galapagos.

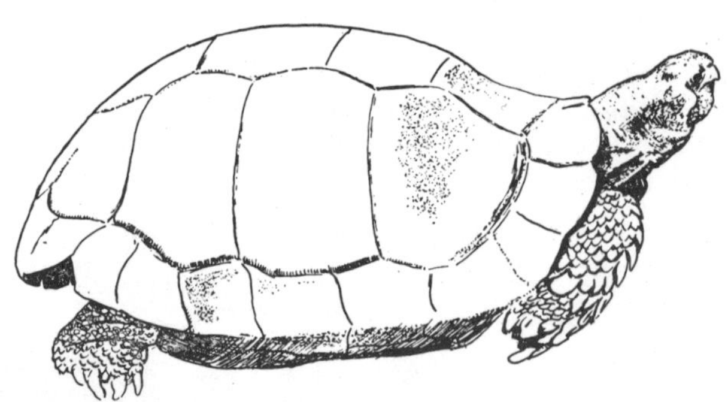

● **RED-FOOTED TORTOISE** *Testudo tabulata*

Also called SOUTH AMERICAN TORTOISE.

Average size 24 inches; largest 36 inches; edible.

Dark brown in color; sometimes black, with a yellow blotch on each shield.

Very abundant in their native land and shipped in numbers to Europe. Essentially a forest dweller, living on a diet of fruit, best liked on the rotted side. In captivity they eat cabbage and lettuce.

Range: Tropical South America.

● **BURMESE BROWN TORTOISE**

Testudo emys

Also called ANAM KAKI.

Average size 24 inches; largest 30 inches; edible.

Distinguished by the depressed shell. Outside margins are serrated. Have spurs, which gives the name "six-footed."

Native of dry forest terrain, feeding on plants and fruit. Apparently do not hibernate, but keep on the go winter and summer. In captivity they prefer carrots and bananas.

Range: Siam, Burma, Sumatra and the Malay Peninsula.

Terrapins

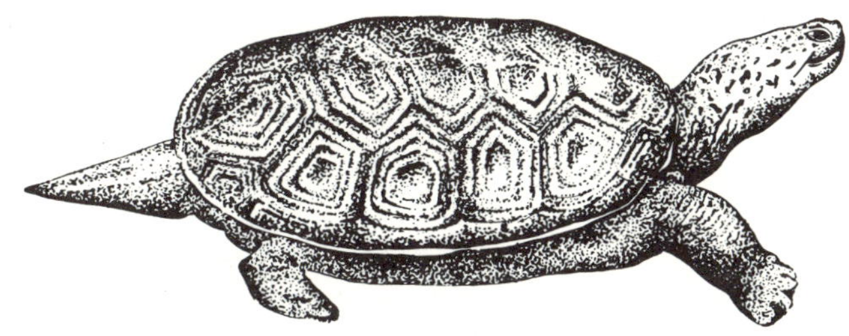

● DIAMOND-BACK TERRAPIN

Malaclemys terrapin

Average size male 4 inches; females grow to 12 inches.

Size discrepancy of sexes is characteristic of the *malaclemys*.

Diamond-shape shields on carapace, head mottled. Almost decimated by gourmets, are now protected by law. Those on the market raised in captivity.

Live mostly in salt or brackish water and feed on shellfish. Very intelligent for turtles. In captivity will answer to call and perform tricks.

Range: Massachusetts to Maryland.

● RED-EARRED TURTLE

Pseudemys s. elegans

Also called MOBILE TERRAPIN.

Average size 8 inches; largest 10½ inches; edible.

Identified by a broad scarlet band on either side of head.

A showy terrapin, much sought after as an epicurean delicacy. Sold in markets under the name "Sliders". Herbivorous usually, but also eat snails, crawfish, tadpoles and frogs. They browse on leaves of aquatic vegetation.

Range: Over a wide area of United States, from Ohio to the Gulf States and west to the Rio Grande.

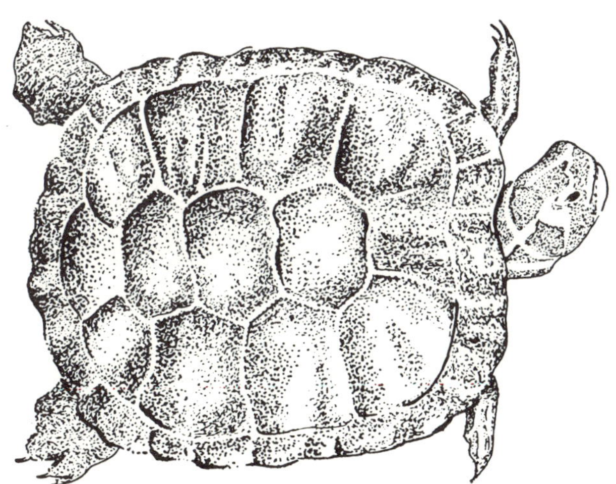

● YELLOW-BELLIED TURTLE

Pseudemys s. scripta

Average size 8 inches; largest 10 inches; edible.

Identified by the wrinkled formation on the upper shell. Also with yellow under portion.

Semi-aquatic and choosing the coastal plains area for the best liked terrain. Prefers marshy area, such as in South Carolina and Virginia coast. They burrow in the mud in winter and come out in Spring thaws.

Range: Eastern coastal states from Virginia to Georgia.

● MAP TURTLE

Malachemys geographica

Also called the GEOGRAPHIC TERRAPIN.

Average size 9 inches; largest 11 inches; edible. Good food.

Olive or brown carapace is marked with a series of yellowish lines resembling geographic boundaries.

At home in deep water throughout the Eastern states. Difficult to catch, as they are particularly wary, taking advantage of deep water.

Range: Throughout the Ohio and Mississippi valleys to the St. Lawrence River and Lake Champlain.

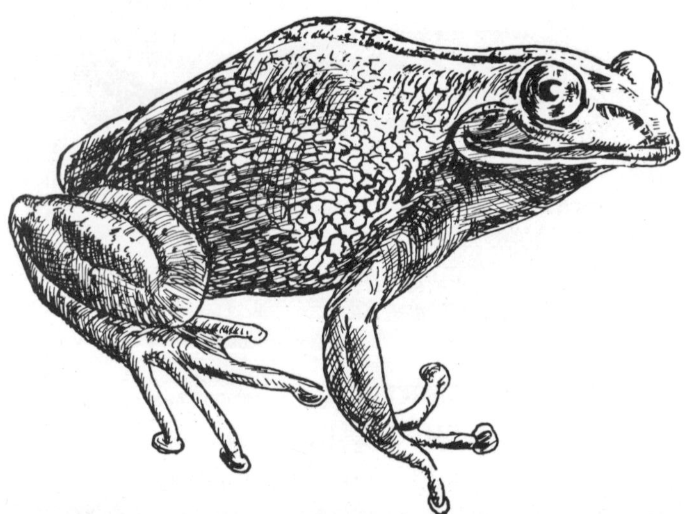

● GIANT TREE FROG
Hyla septentrionalis

Also called CUBAN TREE FROG.

Average size 3 inches; largest 5 inches; harmless.

Usually olive-green, faintly barred with dusky olive. Lower side, dull yellow. Head broad and rounded; eyes large; skin covered with small scattered bumps. Pads on feet are unusually large.

The largest frog in Western Hemishere. Real home is Cuba, although they have somehow migrated to other islands about the Gulf of Mexico. They are found in the Key West Islands, only known area in the United States.

Eat insects, snails and other small frogs. Quite often found around house drain pipes. Usual home is in mangrove trees.

● GIANT FROG
Rana Goliah

Average size 10 inches; largest 12 inches; edible.

Greenish brown with white throat and belly.

The giant of the frog family; largest in the world. At 12 inches in length, this monster towers over the average sized frog like the Empire State building over the home town railroad station.

Has a voice more powerful than a calliope and can be heard for miles. Sometimes mistaken for a steamer's horn.

Range: The swampland of the Cameroons in Africa.

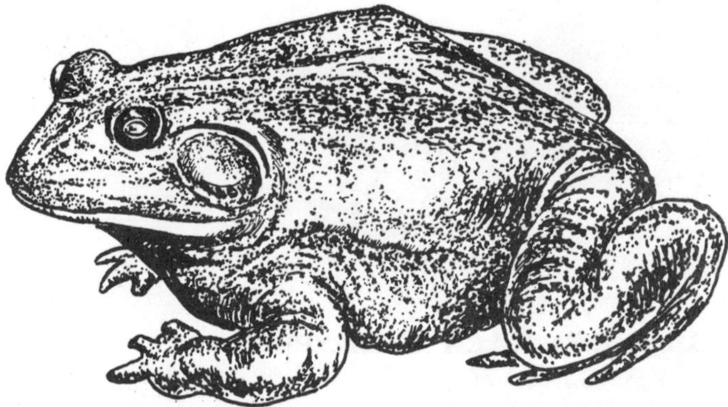

● BULL FROG
Rana catesbeiana

Average size 5 inches; largest 8 inches; harmless. Southern specimens seldom grow over 5 inches and average 3 inches.

Green or greenish-brown with yellow throat; under belly sometimes white and often spotted.

Inhabits the shores and lily pads of lakes and ponds. Has a big deep croaking voice, but seldom joins a duet. Feeds on crayfish mostly and swims powerfully, although only a short distance at a time. Chief enemies are snakes and birds. When snatched by a hawk the scream of anguish sounds terrifying.

Range: Throughout the Western Hemisphere, or from England to Japan. Particularly numerous in America.

● HORNED FROG
Ceratophrys varia

Also called BARKING TOAD.

Average size 5 inches; largest 7 inches; dangerous.

Green and yellow skin with dark green spots. On sides and limbs there are yellow and white dots. The horns are a flexible skin growth.

This ill-tempered and aggressive member of the frog family, will attack and eat anything that can be caught, including his brother. They often catch birds and mice.

When not in the trees, may be found digging into the ground, tossing dirt on his back to offer concealment, the better to leap out after passing game.

Range: Brazil and Argentina.

Giant Toads

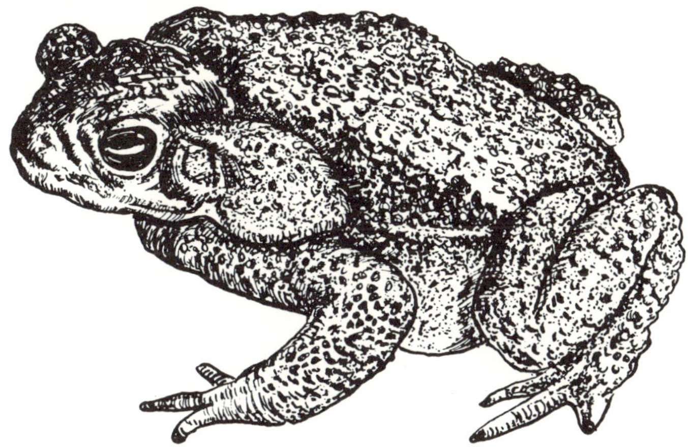

● MARINE TOAD
Bufo marinus

Also called GIANT TOAD.

Average size 4 inches; largest 6 inches; harmless.

Brown skin on back, quite warty and splotched with black.

One of the misnamed of the animal kingdom. The Marine Toad does not live in the sea but far inland. Many years back the scientist Linnaeus received a specimen found on a beach and concluded they were sea-going.

Greatest skill is the catching of mosquitoes. A tongue both quick and long can snatch up 50 mosquitoes a minute from the air. Usually they sit in a puddle or in vegetation, but seldom are found swimming.

Range: Tropical America including Southern Texas.

● AMERICAN TOAD
Bufo americanus

Also called SOUTHERN TOAD.

Average size 3 inches; largest 4½ inches; harmless.

Identified by black-spotted belly.

This is the familiar toad of the gardens and woods. Seen in the grass on lawns and almost everywhere. The song of males on Spring nights is very melodious. Noted for fertility. Females lay 4,000 eggs at a time in ponds or shallow puddles.

Considered a friend of man because of a great appetite for insects, which are harmful to humanity.

Range: Generally distributed throughout the American continent.

● CUBAN TOAD
Bufo empusus

Average size 3 inches; largest 4½ inches; harmless.

Greenish-brown, liberally covered with warts. Exceptionally large eyes.

A typical garden variety of toad found in the island of Cuba. Hops around feeding on insects in the cane fields and about the gardens of the island. Is a prodigious eater and will consume ants, potato bugs and worms as fast as they can be found.

Range: Cuba.

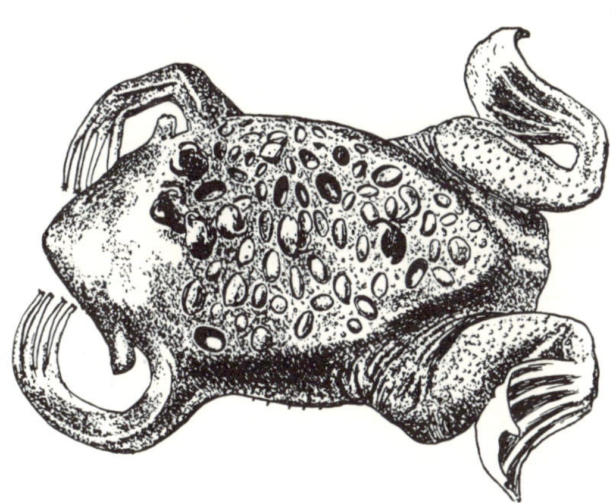

● SURINAM TOAD
Pipa pipa

Average size 3½ inches; largest 5 inches; harmless.

Dark brown above; whitish underparts. Easily identified by egg depressions on back and weird shaped head with tiny pellet-shaped eyes. Tongueless. Sweeps food in with its slender fingers.

The strangest of all reptiles, this creature, considered the ugliest, has the most satisfying relationship of family raising. The male after fertilizing the female, takes the eggs when they are laid and presses them into her back. Here they remain until hatching, when they are dug out, as the tiny hands and feet emerge. All the way it's a co-operative deal.

Range: Brazil, Guianas and Trinidad.

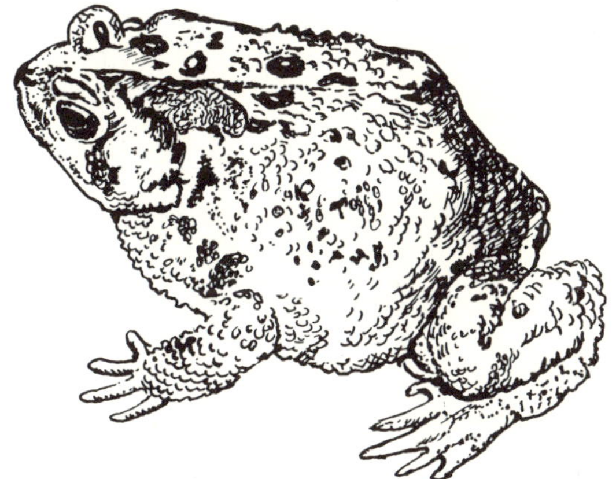

# Unusual Frogs and Toads

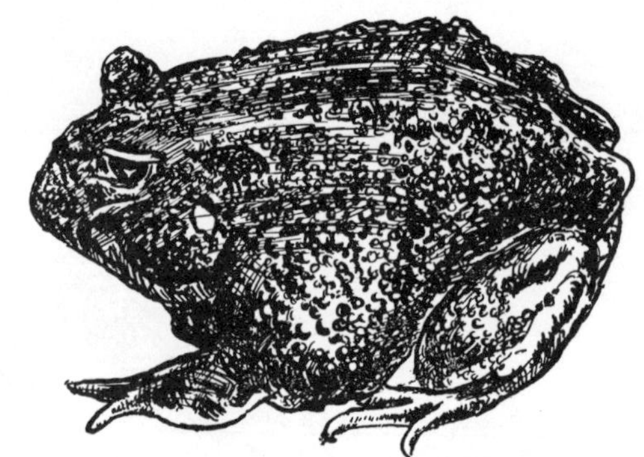

● ORNAMENTED CERATOPHRYS
Ceratophrys ornata

Average size 3 inches; largest 3½ inches; harmless.

Upper surfaces bright green with large reddish-brown, and black-edged markings. Jaws are bright yellow. Upper eyelid raised and pointed.

Burrowing toad, spending most of life beneath the surface. Considered the most beautiful of the species. Has the ability to emit a startling cry, like an infant in mortal fear. Opens mouth wide while screaming loudly.

Feeds on small frogs and mice.

Range: Southern Brazil and the Argentine.

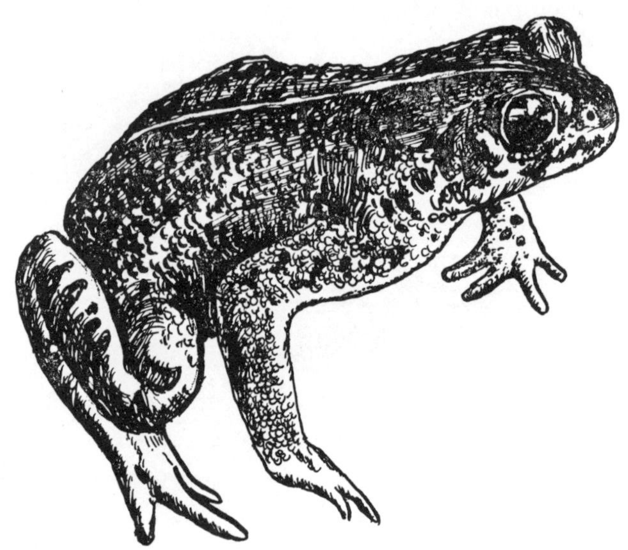

● NATTERJACK TOAD
Bufo calamita

Average size 2 inches; largest 2½ inches; harmless.

Snout short and blunt; legs short; upper parts covered with huge warts. Color of upper surfaces grayish or greenish with brown and olive markings. Some of the large warts are often red. A yellow vertebral line extends along the middle of the back. Lower surfaces, dirty white.

Because of the short limbs, this is one Toad which does not hop. Instead gets under way by running, the body raised slightly from the ground. Usually abundant in and around hills, close to the sea. Likes to burrow.

Usually found in dry sandy terrain.

Range: Northern and Western Europe; Ireland and Scotland.

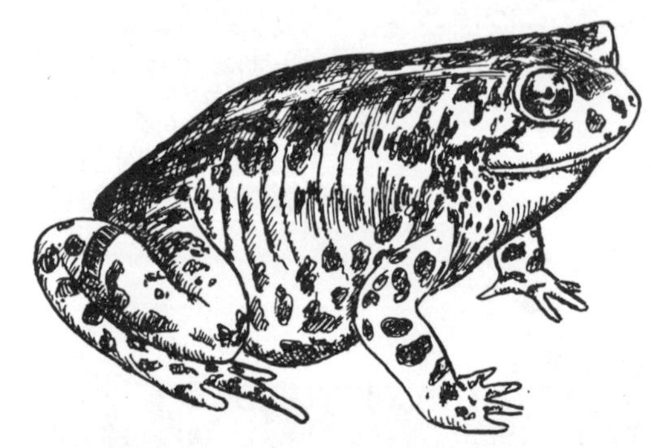

● GREEN TOAD
Bufo viridis

Average size 2½ inches, largest 4 inches; harmless.

Color varies from grayish, yellowish or pinkish above, with irregular shaped blotches, varying from bright green to dark olive, margined with black. A fine yellow vertebral line sometimes present. Back covered with warts of various sizes.

An aquatic toad, much more so than the Common Toad. Also it is a mountain-loving creature, having been found at altitudes of 15,000 feet.

Range: Widely distributed through Central and Southern Europe; also on the islands of the Mediterranean; in North Africa from Morocco to Lower Egypt and in Central Asia to the Himalayas.

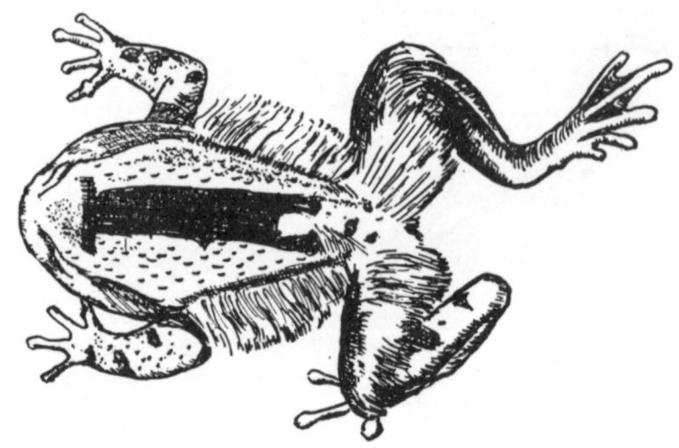

● HAIRY FROG
Astylosternus robustus

Average size 2 inches; largest 3 inches; harmless.

Identified by hair-like appendages on sides and upper thighs.

Rare specimen of the Frog clan, this creature has a covering of fine hairs, used primarily as sense organs. The fuzz somewhat resembles feathers. Not much is known of this species.

Range: South Africa.

Common Frogs

● WHITE'S TREE FROG *Hyla caerulea*

Average size 2½ inches; largest 4 inches; harmless.

Bright green head is very broad; skin smooth and shiny, so much so it gives the impression of being made of wax.

A large species of tree frog, commonly imported to various countries, because of a very hardy constitution. Will eat greedily, all kinds of insects, worms and snails.

Range: Native to Australia.

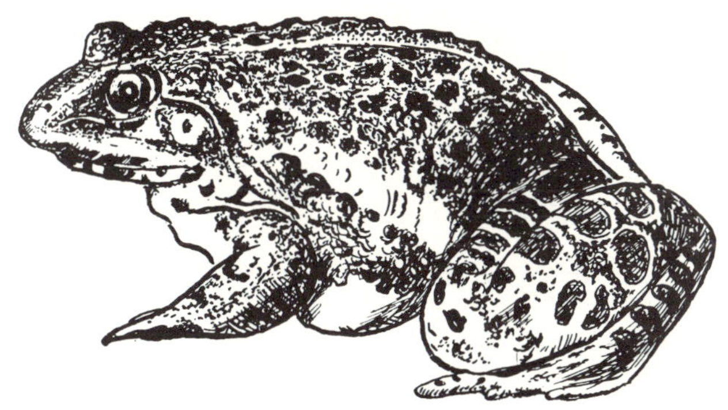

● INDIAN BULL FROG *Rana tigrina*

Also called TIGRINE FROG.

Averge size 4 inches; largest 6 inches; harmless; edible.

Upper parts gray, with dark streaks or spots. Has a pointed and projecting snout.

A Bull Frog of the Orient. Seldom leaves the water. Emits a resounding croak, especially in breeding season. Feed on small birds and mice.

Range: India, Ceylon, the Malay Peninsula and southern China.

● FLORIDA GOPHER FROG *Rana capito aesopus*

Average size 3 inches; largest 6 inches; harmless; edible.

Color varies from pale gray with spots to uniform dark brown. Stout body has many elongated warts.

Most of the year this frog lives in the burrows of the Gopher Tortoise. Seldom does one see them for they are quick to disappear when danger is apparant. They feed principally on small toads.

Range: Only known in Florida.

● AFRICAN BULL FROG *Rana adspersa*

Also called THE SPECKLED FROG.

Average size 5 inches; largest 8 inches; harmless; edible.

Color above is olive, with light vertebral line. Has a shovel-like tubercle on inner side of the foot, for burrowing.

The counterpart of the American Bull Frog, except a bit heavier, which gives the appearance of a toad. Gather in ponds during spring mating season, but most other times remain buried in the ground.

Range: Native of South and East Africa.

Tree Frogs

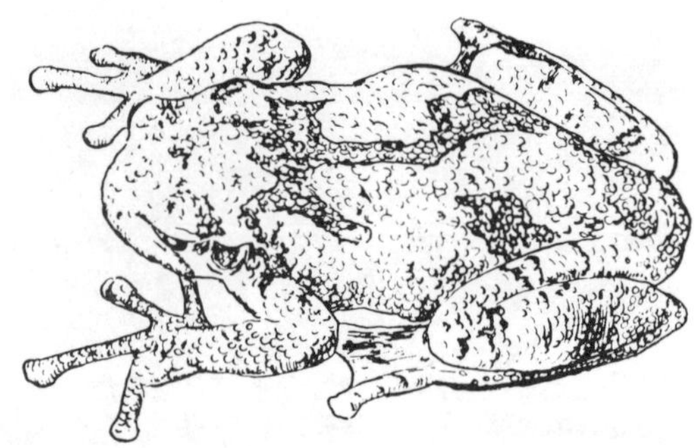

● GRAY TREE FROG
Hyla versicolor

Average size 2 inches; largest 3 inches; harmless.

Ashy-gray sometimes varying to green or brown. Identified by dark band over each eye, star shaped patch on the back; small yellowish patch below the eye; under belly grayish-white, except legs, which are bright orange.

This is the common Tree Frog known throughout the eastern United States. An excellent climber and living most all the time in trees.

Sings on hot sultry Summer nights or on cloudy afternoons which has caused natives of the South to predict rain when they hear this frog's cheerful trilling. Feeds on insects.

Range: Found throughout the Eastern United States, Canada to Florida; west to Kansas; Texas.

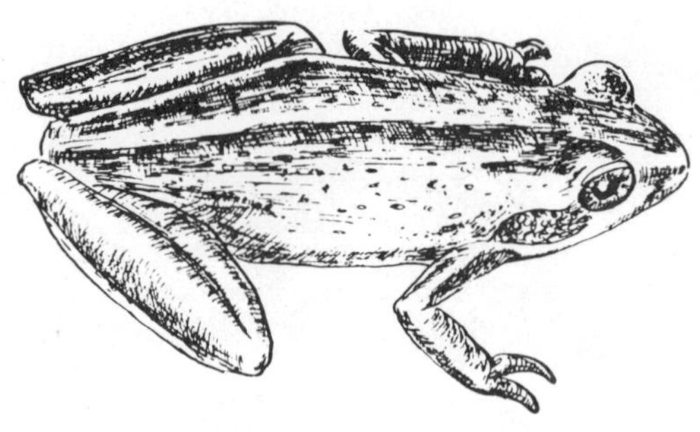

● SQUIRREL TREE FROG
Hyla squirella

Also called HOUSE FROG, SOUTHERN TREE FROG, SCRAPER FROG, RAIN FROG.

Average size 1½ inches; largest 2 inches; harmless.

Changes shades easily from green to orange-yellow. Identified by a dark patch between the eyes and a light line along upper jaw. Lower surface white; orange-yellow on the throat.

An agile tree frog, considered in some ways quicker than a squirrel. Especially active after a rain. Likes to live in trees near a stream, but is sometimes found in cornfields and such dry terrain.

Sounds a call, not loud, pitched to a light trill. Doesn't last long.

Range: From Virginia to Texas.

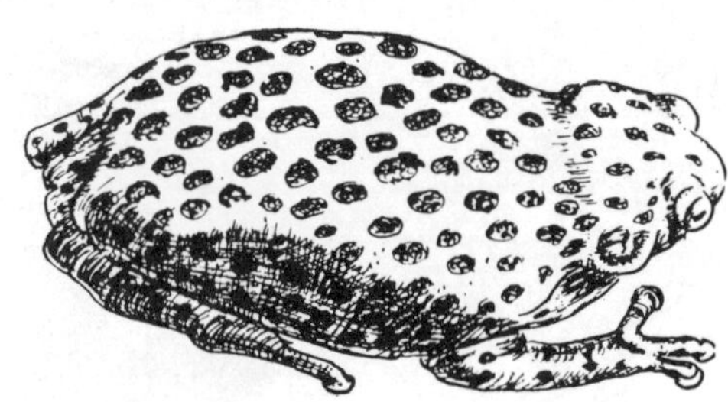

● BARKING TREE FROG
Hyla gratiosa

Average size 2½ inches; largest 3 inches; harmless.

Distinguished by coarse granulated skin; changes colors at will from ash-gray to bright green. Upper surface of body covered with evenly spaced spots, usually encircled with black.

One of largest American frogs. A rare creature and not often captured. Has a deep voice which coming from the tree tops, resembles a barking dog. Likes trees close to water, but spends little time in the water.

Range: Southern coastal regions, from South Carolina to Louisiana.

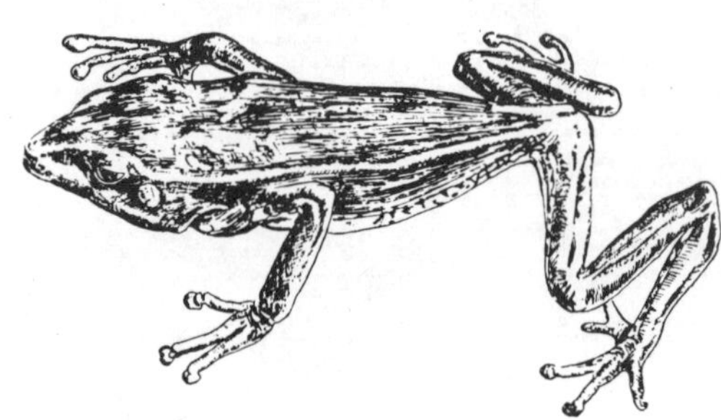

● GREEN TREE FROG
Hyla cinerea

Average size 1½ inches; largest 2 inches; harmless.

Back is shiny and grass green; underparts yellowish-white, turning pinkish on the thighs. When a fly settles nearby, they leap great distances to get it.

One of the most common frogs in America and known throughout Europe and Asia. One branch of this family in Haiti grows to a length of five inches. They are renowned for loud trillings, not considered unpleasant by nature lovers.

Range: Southeastern United States, mostly.

Unusual Toads

● MIDWIFE TOAD
Alytes obstetricans

Average size 2½ inches; largest 3 inches; harmless.

Gray or brown back, smooth, spotted with green or red; underparts are grayish-white . Identified by provision to carry basket of eggs on back.

Probably the best animal mother of the cold blooded creatures. To guard the eggs until they are hatched this toad carries them everywhere. This is not a credit to the feminine sex, however, for the midwife is a male—it's papa.

Mrs. Toad winds the string of eggs around his legs when they are laid and then the expectant father hikes off to some hiding place and takes good care of the eggs until they hatch. Every night he dampens them in water. When they are ready to hatch, he swims slowly in the water while the egg cases dissolve and the little ones swim off.

Range: Southeastern Europe, France, Portugal, to southeastern Holland.

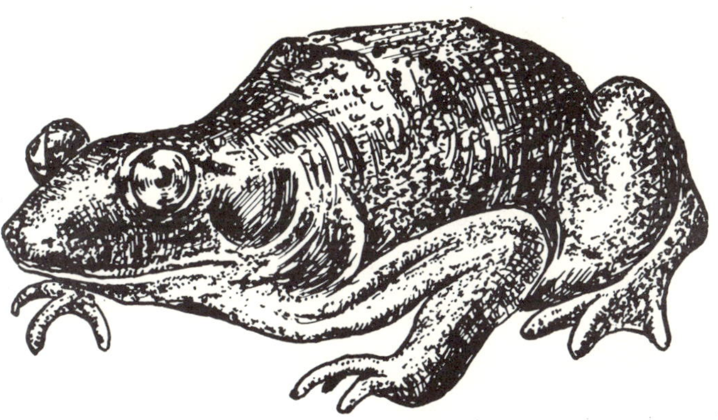

● EASTERN SPADEFOOT TOAD
Scaphiopus holbrooki

Also called HERMIT TOAD, GARLIC TOAD.

Average size 2 inches; largest 3 inches; harmless.

May be green, yellow or ash-brown. Usually looks like a ball of dirt when first seen. Undersides dingy white.

A burrowing toad which spends all its life in the ground. Two efficient diggers on the hind feet can cause the toad to sink right down out of sight.

Some members of this family emit an odor like garlic, when first captured.

Range: Most common in eastern half of the United States.

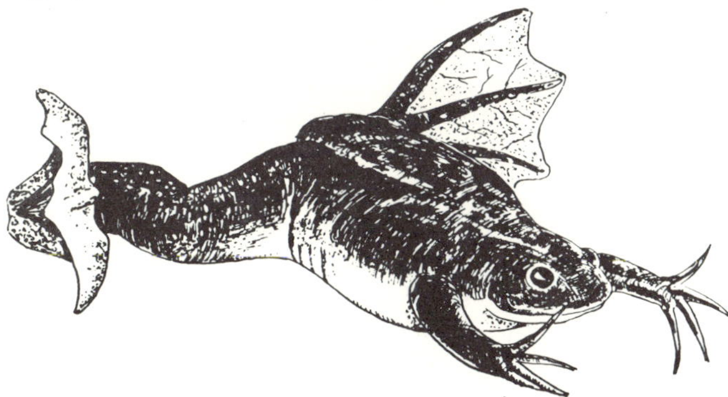

● CLAWED TOAD
Xenopus laevis

Average size 2¼ inches; largest 3 inches; harmless.

Smooth skin, covered with tube-like structures; upper parts olive-brown; belly whitish and sometimes spotted with brown.

Related to the huge Surinam Toad, this creature darts around in ponds and feeds gluttonously. The three claws or spikes on forefeet make for easy capture of insects, especially with large webbed hind feet for propulsion.

The Clawed Toad has been used successfully in pregnancy tests.

Range: Tropical Africa.

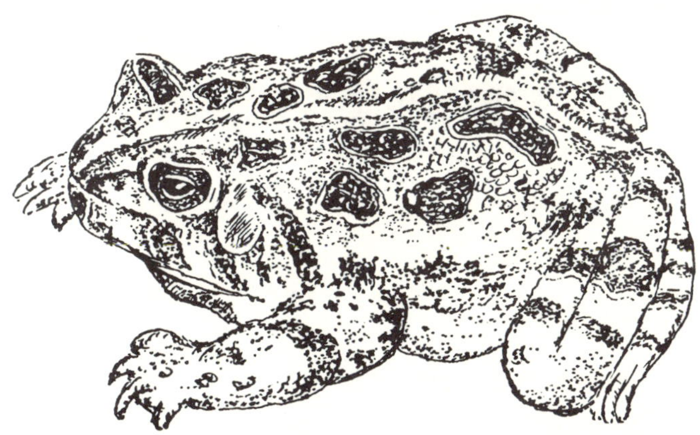

● FOWLER'S TOAD
Bufo woodhousi fowleri

Average size 2½ inches; largest 3¼ inches; harmless.

Identified by unmarked or spotted belly and with two warts in each dorsal spot; no warts on upper surfaces of hind legs.

This toad is different in several respects from the American Toad. One characteristic is the voice which sounds like the bleating of sheep.

Range: Eastern United States.

American Frogs

● **WOOD FROG**

Rana sylvatica

Maximum length 3¼ inches.

A rather decorative little fellow whose colors vary with location. Color may be tan, grayish, pink, orange, copper—but the "robber's mask" patch is always brown. Its call sounds like the quacking of ducks.

Ranges widely from Alaska throughout Canada and south as far as Georgia.

LEOPARD FROG
Rana pipiens

Also called MEADOW FROG.

Average size 3 inches; largest 4 inches; harmless.

Greenish or brownish in color with two rows of rounded dark spots on back. Does not have the orange tint under legs that identifies a Pickerel Frog.

A wanderer of the fields in Summer and likes the streams and ponds in Spring. Widely distributed over Eastern United States. A gutteral note in the voice heard from the male.

Range: Eastern United States.

● **NORTHERN CRICKET FROG**

Acris crepitans

Averge size 1 inch; largest 1¼ inches; harmless.

Have a variety of patterns. Brown and green predominate. Some are marked with red. Identified by a dark triangle between the eyes. Has a short and erratic jump.

Is a member of the tree frog group, although with more terrestrial habits. The call sounds like two pebbles being clicked together, something like the mechanical crickets that small boys use. They like ditches and shallow ponds, when not in trees.

Range: Northeastern United States.

● **PICKEREL FROG**

Rana palustris

Maximum length 3 1/8 inches.

Brown, with two rows of squarish, dark spots on back; bright orange on concealed surfaces of hind legs.

Voice sounds like grunting or snorting and often emitted while under water.

Skins secretes a poison distasteful to enemies.

Range: Eastern United States.

● **MINK FROG**

Rana septentrionalis

Average size 2 inches; largest 3 inches; harmless.

Identified by the odor. When skin is rubbed, a smell is produced not unlike the smell of mink. Resembles a Green Frog a great deal.

A cold country frog, living and preferring cold weather at elevations in excess of 1,000 feet. Inhabit the cold waters of lakes and ponds. Breed late in the season, mostly in July.

Range: Hudson Bay area of Canada to northern New York and New England.

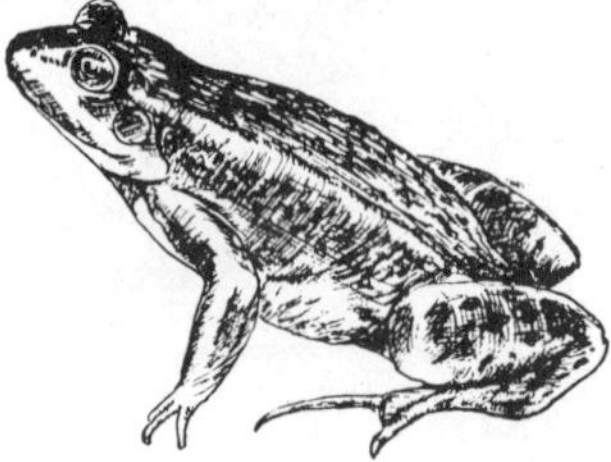

● **CARPENTER FROG**

Rana virgatipes

Also called SPHAGNUM FROG

Average size 2 inches; largest 2⅝ inches; harmless.

Identified by yellowish lines extending backward upon the body from the eyes. There are no dorso-lateral folds. They can jump only a short distance.

These frogs are named because their mating call resembles the pounding of a hammer. A bunch of them sounds like somebody building a house. They like the dark-colored waters of the cranberry and sphagnum bogs.

Range: Mostly found in southern New Jersey.

Index

Index